T0295662

Internal Crisis Communication

We live in a crisis society, with traditional media responding on a minute-by-minute basis on daily, seemingly inevitable, organizational crises. Whether crises have become more prevalent or we're simply more aware of them, they are now of great concern to organizations and crisis management and communication is a priority. Most organizations have a crisis response plan; many have dedicated crisis and security management staff. Yet much of the emphasis has been on action outside of the organization. Neglecting communication between managers and co-workers, they risk poor, inconsistent crisis management and the very real possibility of crisis escalation. Crisis management, like charity, begins in the home.

Internal Crisis Communication is one of the first guides to communication inside organizations, before, during and after a crisis – not just on the acute crisis phase – to provide a complete and holistic guide for managers that will help them manage and contain crises. It includes an in-depth real-life case study, referred to throughout, from the author's own experience, which makes practical application explicit and the methodology clear.

Strengthened by rigorous academic research and tested in real-life crisis situations, the methods included in this book will be invaluable for communication professionals, security officers and crisis managers, as well as valuable reading for students and researchers interested in crisis and risk management.

Mats Heide is professor in strategic communication at Lund University. He is coauthor of *Strategic Communication* (with Jesper Falkheimer, Routledge 2018) and co-editor of *Strategic Communication, Social Media and Democracy* (Routledge 2016). Heide has published 12 books in Swedish on internal communication, crisis communication and strategic communication.

Charlotte Simonsson is senior lecturer in strategic communication at Lund University. She is former head of the Department of Strategic Communication at Lund University and has a career as a communication consultant. Simonsson has published several books in Swedish on internal communication, leadership and organizational communication.

Internal Crisis Communication

Crisis Awareness, Leadership and Coworkership

Mats Heide and Charlotte Simonsson

LONDON AND NEW YORK

First published 2019
by Routledge
2 Park Square, Milton Park, Abingdon, Oxon OX14 4RN

and by Routledge
52 Vanderbilt Avenue, New York, NY 10017

Routledge is an imprint of the Taylor & Francis Group, an informa business

British Library Cataloguing-in-Publication Data
A catalogue record for this book is available from the British Library

Library of Congress Cataloging-in-Publication Data
A catalog record has been requested for this book

ISBN: 978-1-138-35407-4 (hbk)
ISBN: 978-0-429-42504-2 (ebk)

Typeset in Celeste and Optima
by Apex CoVantage, LLC

MIX
Paper from
responsible sources
FSC
www.fsc.org   FSC™ C013985

Printed in the United Kingdom
by Henry Ling Limited

Contents

About the authors

Mats Heide (PhD, Lund University, 2002), is professor in strategic communication at the Department of Strategic Communication, Lund University, Campus Helsingborg. His research interests are strategic communication in general, and more specifically crisis communication, change communication and organizational learning. Heide has coauthored 12 books (in Swedish) and one international textbook together with Jesper Falkheimer (*Strategic Communication: An Introduction*, Routledge, 2018). Heide is also co-editor of *Strategic Communication, Social Media and Democracy: The Challenge of the Digital Naturals* (with Coombs, Falkheimer & Young, Routledge, 2015). His work is published in *Corporate Communications: An International Journal*, the *International Journal of Strategic Communication*, the *Journal of Contingencies and Crisis Communication*, *Public Relations Inquiry* and *Public Relations Review*. Heide is also published in edited volumes such as *Public Relations and Social Theory* (2009), the *Handbook of Crisis Management* (with Jesper Falkheimer, 2010), *Encyclopedia of Public Relations II* (2013), *Handbook of Crisis Management* (2013), *Routledge Handbook of Strategic Communication* (with Jesper Falkheimer, Routledge 2014), *Public Relations: Critical Concepts in Media and Cultural Studies* (with Jesper Falkheimer, Routledge 2014), the *Encyclopedia of Quality and the Service Economy* (2014), the *Handbook of Critical Public Relations* (with Jesper Falkheimer, Routledge 2015), the *Encyclopedia of Strategic Communication* (2018), the *Handbook of Communication Engagement* (with Charlotte Simonsson, 2018), the *Handbook of Public Sector Communication* (with Charlotte Simonsson, 2019) and *Public Relations and Social Theory* (2019).

Charlotte Simonsson (PhD, Lund University, 2002), is assistant professor in strategic communication. Charlotte has served as the head of the Department of Strategic Communication at Lund University and has a background as a senior consultant within strategic communication. Her main research interests are crisis communication, change communication, leadership communication and roles and practices of communication professionals. At present, she is engaged in the research project *The Communicative Organization* with the purpose to clarify how communication contributes to value creation and organizational goal accomplishment. Simonsson is the author of several books in Swedish and her work is published in journals such as the *International Journal of Strategic Communication, Corporate Communications: An International Journal,* the *Journal of Communication Management, Public Relations Inquiry* and *Public Relations Review.* Simonsson is also published in edited volumes such as the *Encyclopedia of Strategic Communication* (2018), the *Handbook of Communication Engagement* (with Mats Heide, 2018) and the *Handbook of Public Sector Communication* (with Mats Heide, 2019).

Foreword

ORGANIZATIONAL CRISES have become increasingly typical and extensive in the complex society of today. Crises are no longer seen as an unusual or peripheral occurrence but are, instead, perceived as an integral and inevitable part of an organization's existence. As a result, interest in crisis management and crisis communication has increased in the past few decades among researchers and practitioners alike. That which has been of most interest to researchers and practitioners is how to respond to a crisis and how to communicate outwards during the most intensive phase of a crisis. This book, however, will take the opposite view and focuses on communication from an internal perspective, between the managers and co-workers situated in the middle of the crisis. The response an organization has to a crisis and their communication with external groups is largely a result of internal communication processes, which makes its absence from previous research surprising. Traditionally, crisis research has been focused on the most acute and intensive phase of the crisis – the emergency situation. In this book, we are instead taking up the discussion from a broader, more development-oriented perspective. This means that we are not only interested in what happens during the crisis but also in what happens both before and after the crisis occurs. We are also looking at how organizations, communications and leadership can be developed in order to avoid and manage crises, as well as in order to increase learning in crisis situations.

The book *Internal Crisis Communication: Crisis Awareness, Leadership and Coworkership* is the first book that focuses on the internal aspects of crisis communication. As far as we know, there are no international books written on this topic from a holistic perspective. So far, there is a master's thesis published as a book (Kukule, 2014), which defines internal crisis communication as crises that happens within an organization. There is also a PhD thesis on internal crisis communication published by Young (2016). He takes a managerial perspective on how two-way symmetrical and transparent communication can be used to enforce co-workers to improve organizational resilience.

Research to date on internal crisis communication is rather limited, but we can see an increasing interest in this area among international researchers (see the review in Chapter 3). The purpose of this book is to introduce, highlight and discuss internal crisis communication based on recent research. Our theoretical discussions in this book are supplemented with empirical material from a 3-year research project at a Swedish University Hospital. While we will give some examples from the study, they have a general nature, as this book is not intended to focus on healthcare *per se*.

We have had the privilege of researching internal crisis communication for 3 years. Our research has been a part of the research project "Internal Crisis Communication: Strategies and Methods for Public Organizations' Internal Crisis Management" funded by the Swedish Civil Contingencies Agency. The project was aimed at contributing new knowledge, strategies and methods to public organizations' work on internal crisis communication.

We would like to express our sincere gratitude to the Swedish Civil Contingencies Agency, which made this research possible. We would also like to thank Skåne University Hospital in Lund and Malmö, Sweden, and all co-workers we interviewed as part of this project. Without your engagement, reflections and wisdom this project would not have been possible to complete. We would also like to thank the former student at our international master's program in strategic communication, Clara Bartlett, for her careful and efficient translation of the Swedish book manuscript.

Mats Heide & Charlotte Simonsson
April 2019

Introduction

IT IS OFTEN claimed that we live in a crisis society. Be it the newspapers, radio, TV, or Internet, you can find constant reports of the dangers and threats that today's societies and citizens face. Just as often you will find reports in the mass media of corporations and public and nonprofit organization's crisis. Reporting and discussions on organizational crises are often also found on social media, not least on Facebook. With increasing globalization and internationalization, companies are acting in new markets with special legal, technical, environmental and logistical conditions, thereby increasing their risk of facing a crisis. The increased complexity that characterizes modern society leads to uncertainty and ambiguity, making it increasingly difficult to predict the future and find clear answers.

Some examples of larger, internationally well-known organizational crisis are the following:

- *Union Carbide's* gas leak in Bhopal: In December 1984, a gas leak from a pesticide factory owned by Union Carbide ravaged the Indian city Bhopal. More than 500,000 people were exposed to gas, and the accident was considered the world's largest industrial disaster. It is unclear how many died, but many thousands suffered severe injuries. The debate on what caused this disaster is still ongoing, but substandard factory design, a lack of maintenance, poor personnel policies and budget cutbacks are all considered to have played a role.
- *Nestlé's* aggressive marketing of breast milk formula: Since 1977, a number of countries have decided to boycott Nestlé as a result of its marketing strategies for breast milk formula in poor countries,

1

which are considered to violate the World Health Organization's ethical rules. Nestlé is critiqued for providing free testing and biased advertising to encourage mothers to use formula instead of breast-feeding, which critics argue poses a danger to children's health. Nestlé is not the only company being criticized for its unethical marketing tactics, but as it is a group with extremely large market shares, criticism against them has been especially sincere.

- *Findus*'s ground beef scandal: On January 15, 2013, the Irish counterpart to the Food and Drug Administration found that there was horse and pig meat DNA in frozen burgers. The scandal reached several countries. On February 6, it came out that Findus's deep-frozen one-portion lasagna, manufactured by the French company Comigel, contained horsemeat. The European distributor networks are very complex, but it was finally found that this meat came from a Romanian manufacturer. Many consider Findus to have been successful in its crisis management and crisis communication, even though its head of communications was not a part of the process. Among other things, Findus acted proactively and managed to restore the company's reputation (read more about the case in Falkheimer & Heide, 2015).

Traditionally, risks and crisis have been perceived as something objective and measurable. It has been assumed that they exist and occur outside or inside an organization and that they harm the organization in various ways. Contemporary research, however, points to the fact that it is not that simple. Individuals' and organizations' perceptions of what constitutes a crisis depends on their own values, norms, interests, education, experiences and self-image (Renn, 1992). If you experience a situation or circumstance as a risk or a crisis, you will undoubtedly also act on the basis of that perception. You could even say that the question, "What is a risk?" is wrongly put. So, argue Boholm and Corvellec (2011), who say that the better question to ask is, "How do people understand something to be a risk?" (in Chapter 1 on page 5 we elaborate on the difference between risk and crisis).

Crises can thus be seen as a question of perception and social construction. This clearly does not mean that the number of deaths in the Tylenol crisis (see page 20) or the Bhopal disaster is a social construction but, rather, that how we perceive the management of the crisis and how we act is a result of social and communicative interactions.

Crisis management and crisis communication are thus inseparable from one another. Identifying, preparing for, managing and proceeding after a crisis is largely about interpreting information and communicating with a number of individuals and groups.

Large focus on the external perspective

The well-known German sociologist Ulrich Beck (1992) claims that we live in a risk society. In this society, organizations are increasingly engaged in risk management to map and manage different types of risks. According to Beck, this increased risk management is a consequence of the negative effects of industrial society; industrialism's modern society was aimed at constantly trying to improve the economy and living conditions of people by mastering nature. Mastering soil, precious metals, wind and the sun, to name a few, has, in turn, created many risks for today's society.

It is difficult to say whether it is actually risks and crises that have increased over time or if it is merely reports of them. Crises have, in any case, become increasingly important and received more attention in society and organizations alike. As a consequence, crisis awareness has increased amongst many leaders. Most organizations have, to a varying degree, a crisis preparedness and crisis plan. Many organizations have a chief of safety or the like, who is responsible for managing risks and crisis. What is remarkable about this, however, is that this crisis preparedness is usually aimed at external actors and external communication. The co-workers and the internal perspective are often left in the dark. Johansen, Aggerholm, and Frandsen (2012) found in a survey that 67 percent of Danish organizations (the sample consisted of both private and public organizations) have a policy in place for their external crisis communication, while only 31 percent have a corresponding internal communications policy. Their survey also indicated that co-workers are primarily regarded as recipients of information, and not as ambassadors or initiators of communication in the crisis context.

Even within research, most of the interest has been directed at external factors and external communication. This can be explained by, for example, the fact that the majority of researchers in the field of crisis communication have their background in public relations, which are mainly aimed at external communication (Heide, 2013). Another explanation is that the external world is more visible and reported on in the mass media. The external perspective is therefore prioritized as the effects are the quickest and often the most visible. In sum, there has been too much focus on the external aspects of crisis management and crisis communication. We want to remedy this with this book, where we focus exclusively on an internal perspective on crises and crisis communication.

The important internal perspective

In the past few years, researchers (e.g., D. R. Gilpin & Murphy, 2008; Johansen et al., 2012; Mazzei, 2010; Mazzei, Kim, & Dell'Oro, 2012; Taylor, 2010) have started becoming interested in internal crisis communications. Some researchers, such as Taylor (2010), argue that organizations' internal processes, relations and communication need to be studied in order for research on crisis communication to be able to further develop. Recent research also emphasizes that attention should be given to more than just the acute phase of a crisis: the pre- and post-crisis phases are just as important.

When are organizational crises important to highlight and understand from within? First, it is not always clear exactly when a crisis arises. Contemporary research points out, as mentioned earlier, that crisis is in many ways about perception and perspective. It is estimated that as many as three quarters of all crises do not occur suddenly, but instead develop progressively (see Millar, 2004). Crises are usually preceded by deviations and anomalies that signal that things are not going as intended (Turner, 1976), and these deviations can be important signals that the system is collapsing (Christianson, Sutcliffe, Miller, & Iwashyna, 2011). Thus, whether or not an event is classified as a threat, a risk or a crisis and the actions that follow are determined by peoples' perceptions and interpretations (Boin, 't Hart, Stern, & Sundelius, 2005; Weick, 1993). Another explanation is that people act on the basis of the understanding they have of a situation. Organizations' responses to crises are a direct result of complex internal interpretation processes and communication between co-workers.

Without a doubt, the actors that are most important in determining whether or not an organization is successful in its crisis management and communication is its co-workers (Mercer & Kapcio, 2006). Co-workers are important before, during and after a crisis. It is they who can detect weak signals of changes in and outside the organization, who interpret the signals and react, and who therefore can avoid or dampen the effects of a crisis (Weick & Sutcliffe, 2007). Co-workers often have extensive networks, both internally and externally and thus long tentacles that make them good signal detectives for the organization. These signals may include small changes in the production process or even tampering/sabotage that co-workers are able to notice.

In addition, co-workers have an important role to play once the crisis is a fact. Co-workers are the front end of an organization and are the point of contact for a number of external persons, for example, suppliers, customers and patients. The image that co-workers give obviously affects the external perception of the crisis, and they represent an important asset as ambassadors. In modern strategic research, researchers have departed from the strong focus on the higher levels of leadership and management, as their grandiose strategic plans have little to do with how the strategies are transformed into action. It is only when the strategies that are developed and formulated by management have been communicated, interpreted, negotiated and put into practice that the strategies become interesting to study (see, e.g., Balogun, Best, & Lê, 2015; Kopaneva, 2015). Co-workers themselves are also an important target group during a crisis. When an organization is in crisis, co-workers need information and communication in order to understand and feel secure in what is happening.

Finally, the co-workers are important in the phase following a crisis, when the organization is trying to learn from the event. Co-workers' experiences are crucial for creating new knowledge and action strategies after a crisis, thus creating better opportunities for avoiding future crises (Falkheimer, Heide, & Larsson, 2009). The internal processes are linked to the results of an organization's crisis measures, and they directly affect the surrounding community.

Something exceptional or integrated into development?

This book is geared toward long, complex crises. Of course, there is a big difference between minor crises that suddenly spring up and can be quickly resolved and longer, all-encompassing crises that include lost legitimacy and reputation for the organization as well as adjusting key values, ideas and approaches within the organization. Persistent crises with a high degree of ambiguity and uncertainty also place greater demands on internal communication. Such crises are considerably more complex and require a strategic and long-term crisis perspective in order to be managed successfully. A continuous problem in many organizations is that the strategic perspective on crisis management is lacking; there is too much focus on the "here and now" during the crisis. Organizations tend to effectively act like firefighters, trying to extinguish the fire as fast as possible in the wake of a crisis.

The French crisis researcher Roux-Dufort (2007) puts forward similar criticisms of crisis research, which he believes has an overly limited focus on the exceptional, nonnormal situation and is thus reduced to a study of "exception management." Crisis research has been too oriented toward dealing with surprises, disturbances and emergencies and has therefore not contributed to knowledge about how organizations work or how they can be developed to better deal with crises. Roux-Dufort advocates approaching organizational theories and viewing crises as a long incubation process starting well before the triggering event. We share this view and have therefore chosen to highlight organizational theories and internal communication as an important part of dealing with crises before, during and after they occur.

An organizational theory that is central to this book is *High Reliability Organizations* – HROs. These kinds of organizations are often raised as role models for other organizations in terms of long-term success and management of risks and crises. HROs are characterized by the importance of avoiding risks, disasters and crises by paying attention to minor discrepancies and mistakes (Weick & Sutcliffe, 2007; Weick, Sutcliffe, & Obstfeld, 1999). Furthermore, HROs are characterized by a high degree of flexibility and focus on learning and development (Ruchlin, Dubbs, & Callahan, 2004; Sutcliffe, 2011). Such organizations are proactive and strategic in their crisis management. Examples of organizations that often work like HROs are hospitals, airports, research companies and nuclear power plants. Their operations and technology are precarious, and there are many potential risk factors. Serious failures and mistakes would have dangerous consequences, and their social and political environment does not allow for these mistakes to occur.

Case organization

As mentioned in the Foreword, we are going to present certain results and examples from a qualitative case study of a Swedish university hospital – conducted from the spring of 2011 until the summer of 2013. The hospital is a complex social and technical system, with more than 100 specialist fields within the organization and where assistant nurses, nurses and doctors make up the largest working group. The organization has just over 12,000 individuals employed. This makes the university hospital the third largest of Sweden's seven university hospitals.

We chose to study the university hospital as it is somewhat of an extreme case. Researchers often choose to study organizations where the object of study has a wide range and where there is a lengthy experience of the phenomenon. The university hospital presents particularly good conditions for studying crisis. The hospital is a very important part of society, and it is therefore vital that the organization has a well-developed and effective crisis communication. Questions of safety, risks and crisis are of highest priority at the hospital. Possible crises at the organization are trust crises (e.g., lack of trust in management), medical crises (e.g., a new flu, patient safety) and technical crises (e.g., computer systems, medical devices). The university hospital is also an example of a so-called service organization, where co-workers' direct communication with patients, relatives and other groups is of great importance to the organization's ability to handle crises that are often of major social relevance. For example, in connection with flu epidemics, the co-workers' perceptions and opinions are hugely important to the population's propensity to get vaccinated.

The university hospital also presents itself as an interesting case study as it, in some respects, can be seen as an "HRO," which places great energy and resources on discovering and avoiding crises. This is especially true for medical operations, the nature of which presupposes that risks, mistakes and failure are analyzed and discussed in order to hopefully learn and avoid similar situations in the future.

The university hospital is a relatively new organization. It was formed on January 1, 2010, through a merger of Lund University Hospital and Malmö University Hospital. The time between the decision being made by politicians until the merger went into effect was unusually short: the proposal was first presented in October 2009, while the formal decision was made in November. The merger went into effect on January 1, 2010, which meant that the communications department had only five weeks to carry out the most important work once the decision was made. The communication professionals had, however, already begun their work at the end of October to win time.

The merger between the two hospitals has been met by protest from both external groups and hospital staff. As a consequence of the merger, many specialists and clinics have been moved to one place in order to accumulate expertise. This has, in turn, meant that many personnel have been geographically displaced and that many patients have had to travel longer to get to their clinics; Lund and Malmö are, however, no more than 20 kilometers apart. As always when mergers go through, there were challenges and a bit of wear and tear to face in combining the two organization's cultures. Different experiences, approaches, ideal models, routines and so forth suddenly needed to be coordinated. Some interviewees described a power camp, where Lund stood for the traditional and academic and Malmö for the modern and patient-oriented.

The starting point for our research project was that the boundary between organizational changes and organizational crises is quite diffuse. Many co-workers experienced this merger as a crisis situation and continued to do so long after. Within research, crisis communication and change communication have developed in parallel as two different research fields without much contact between one another, even though these two areas have a lot in common. Both changes and crises bring about high levels of confusion and insecurity among the co-workers, and extra communication is needed to create meaning and understanding that will enable us to handle the situations.

Target group for the book

This book's primary target group is students who are interested in organizational crisis, communication and leaders, for example, within strategic communication, media and communication, sociology, organizational psychology, political science and business administration. The book is also aimed toward practitioners who are affected by and work with crisis management and crisis communication, for example, communicators, safety managers, human resource administrators and managers at differing levels in the organization.

This book not only strives for reflection and innovation but also offers a number of practical solutions. Our ambition is to present theories and concrete examples that can serve as tools and inspiration to develop internal crisis communication. The reader who expects unequivocal and simple advice on how to handle crises internally may be disappointed. Complex crises, however, rarely have a simple or given solution, and we think it is more fruitful to try to visualize and increase understanding for exactly that – the complex and multifaceted.

Chapters of the book

In this Introduction, we have painted a starting point and the purpose of this book with broad strokes. The chapters are as follows:

Chapter 1 – "Crises and communication" – deals with a number of concepts that are central to the book – crisis, risk and organizational crises. In this chapter we also present the different phases of the crisis and previous research in the areas of crisis management and crisis communication.

Chapter 2 – "Perspectives on crises and crisis communication" – presents two overall perspectives: the narrow, information-oriented perspective and the broad, meaning-oriented perspective. In this chapter, we discuss what these perspectives mean for our view of crises and crisis communication in research, and we provide examples of how the perspectives are reflected in crisis management in practice.

Chapter 3 – "Internal crisis communication" – gives a definition of internal crisis communication as well as a review of previous research on the internal facets of an organization's crisis communication. We also present a categorization of the different goals of internal crisis communication and which type of communication is important in the various phases of the crisis.

Chapter 4 – "Leaders and co-workers – perspectives and roles" – is about leadership in connection with crises. In research, as well as in society as a whole, great confidence has been placed in leaders as powerful individuals who can heroically manage the crisis. However, more recent research promotes leadership as a relational, reciprocal process. In line with this development, we not only discuss managers and communicative role, but we also consider co-workers and their communication.

Chapter 5 – "Anticipation – the art of looking for weak signals" – focuses on the importance of organizations constantly searching for signs, signals or changes that could lead to a crisis. Here we place the emphasis on discussing deviation management as a part of an organization's crisis management.

Chapter 6 – "Resilience – the art of managing crisis and learning" – highlights the importance of organizations being resilient, that is, having the ability to handle and recover from a crisis.

Organizational learning, or the formation of new knowledge from a crisis that can be used to avoid and handle future crises, is also closely connected to resilience. Both resilience and learning are crucial for an organization's survival and long-term success.

Chapter 7 – "What can we learn, and how?" – discusses the importance of control and planning versus flexibility and improvisation. In order to cope with the complexities of today's organizations, we often have to deal with a series of paradoxes wherein we need to do both and not either/or. In this final chapter, we also present a series of practical advice on internal crisis communication linked to the different phases of the crisis: pre, during and post.

Chapter 1

Crises and communication

THE COMING CHAPTER lays the groundwork for this book. We discuss the concepts of crisis, risk, organizational crises and crisis communication as a field of research and two perspectives within this field.

Crises

Crises can be regarded both as something negative and catastrophic and as a turning point, and also as a chance to develop and learn. This applies across the board, from society and organizations, all the way down to individuals. A crisis can be a turning point, in which important decisions must be made and pervasive ways of thinking and acting are challenged and ultimately need to be changed. Crises can therefore be seen as an enabler and an opportunity for development.

If you ask someone to describe and define a crisis, the definition you are given is most often the sort of crisis that people experience themselves, meaning the different sorts of "life crises" that everyone goes through at one point or another in his or her life. Life crises can be anything from illness to unemployment, financial hardships, the passing of a loved one, bullying, divorce and everything in between. In this book we are focusing solely on organizational crises, although that is not to say that they are isolated from crises on an individual or societal level (see Figure 1.1). Organizational crises affect co-workers and their relatives, suppliers, owners and customers. Furthermore, some major organizational crises may have major repercussion in society and in the places where the organizations are located. This could entail closures due to financial crises, and as a result, local residents may lose their jobs and the opportunity to support themselves and their

Figure 1.1 Who can be affected by the crisis?

*Source:*Vigsø (2015).

families. Co-workers often end up in life crises because of their sud-denly changed life situation, which can negatively affect their identity (Who am I really?) and self-esteem (I'm worthless!). Society as a whole can also be severely affected by, for example, a major discharge or tech-nical failure in traffic management and traffic monitoring systems for trains. Crises can thus be placed on a scale depending on who they affect (Vigsø, 2015).

The Swedish encyclopedia *Nationalencyklopedin* (www.ne.se) gives six different explanations for the word crisis, all with their own meanings:

- Individual life crises. This entry is the longest, and it describes the psychological crisis that people go through when they find them-selves in a situation that they cannot handle without risking major mental illness. A normal crisis path, divided into four phases, is described as follows: the shock phase, the reaction phase, the pro-cessing phase and the reorientation phase.
- The turning point in a course of illness.
- The moment when there is a sudden and drastic change in the econ-omy, often due to decreasing demand or increasing costs within a particular industry.
- The Swedish nonprofit organization KRIS (in English, CRISIS) – Criminals Return Into Society.
- A Javanese ceremonial, double-edged dagger.
- The Swedish culture journal *Kris* (in English, *Crisis*) that was in print between 1977 and 1997.

The first three entries are the only ones that are connected to our typi-cal associations to the word crisis. The lexical definition of the word *crisis* is a *critical turning point*, which is in line with the first three entries in *Nationalencyklopedin*.

The word *crisis* originates from the Greek word *krisis*, which means "decisive moment," "separation," "judgment" and "verdict." In other words, a situation that we call a crisis entails a serious challenge that requires extra effort, resources and the energy of individuals, organizations and communities to be managed and, in the best of circumstances, resolved. Crises are usually associated with a threat to things of great value, such as life, property, safety, health and psychological stability (Sellnow & Seeger, 2013).

The concept of crisis does not in and of itself mean negative or destructive, but rather, it means challenging. Researchers such as Berger and Luckmann (1966) describe crises as a dissolution of reality, or a situation wherein that which is "normal" no longer exists. In contrast, we have all been fed the negative aspects of crises by our friends' personal accounts of crises, as well as by the constant attention that the mass media places on reporting different types of crises. Focusing on crises is a natural part of the so-called media logic that sociologists David Altheide and Robert Snow (1979) have coined. According to media logic, reporters oversimplify and place an emphasis on personalization and dramatization as a result of strong competition for attention. Journalists are happy to report on, for example, celebrities' miserable divorces, corporate trust crises and different sorts of scare tactics, such as articles saying we need to avoid palm oil, sugar, fat, cell phones and so on.

In this book we choose to view crises as a turning point that presents opportunities. This is in line with the Chinese interpretation of crises, which, according to the Chinese symbol for *crises*, can be interpreted as renewal and new order. In Chinese, *crisis* is written with the two characters *wēi* and *jī* (see Figure 1.2). The first character can be translated into "danger," and the second can be equated with "crucial moment" or "starting point." The Chinese symbol for crisis therefore

Figure 1.2 The Chinese characters for crisis

includes both the positive and the negative, thus giving a slightly better and more balanced view of what crisis means.

In other words, there is an inherent contrast in the concept of crisis: destruction and opportunity (Gilpin & Murphy, 2008). Seeger, Sellnow, and Ulmer (2003) state that

> [c]risis is part of the natural organizational process, purging system elements that are outdated and inappropriate and creating new and unexpected opportunities for development and change, growth, evolution, and renewal.
>
> (p. 7)

Thus, an organization that has undergone a crisis, and thereafter reflected, discussed, transformed and taken in new lessons and experiences, is better equipped to handle future changes and has a higher competitive strength in the market.

We do not have the space to discuss all the aspects of a crisis and do not further discuss individual and societal crises in this book. All the rest of our attention is placed on *organizational crises*.

Organizations and crises

Crises are so normal that organizations should be wondering about *when*, not *if*, they are going to occur. Bozeman (2011, p. 120) is even a bit dramatic in saying that "[b]ad things happen in and to organizations." Mistakes and accidents that can lead to a crisis happen each and every day in organizations, and organizational management cannot afford to say, "It could never happen here" (Coombs, 2006, p. 4). It's human nature to ignore threats and risks, and organizations therefore need to have risk and crisis awareness systems in place, if they want to be successful in the long run.

The world we live in today is increasingly global and complex, where systems are closely connected, and organizations' operations transcend geographical and temporal borders. It is therefore increasingly common to talk about *transboundary crises* (Ansell, Boin, & Keller, 2010), which involve organizations, politicians and public organizations in many different countries. Beck (1992) was early in saying that more and more crises are transboundary crises, such as the nuclear accident in Chernobyl, where the fallout was long-reaching and had severe consequences for many people, even those far from the city.

Another clear example of a transboundary crisis is the Muhammad drawings, which affected the dairy company Arla's operations in Arab countries and had major political consequences. This crisis began in October 2005, when the Danish newspaper *Jyllands-Posten* published twelve caricatures of the Islamic prophet Muhammad, with the cited intention of contributing to the debate about self-censorship in Denmark. The publication of these caricatures provoked the ambassadors for 11 Muslim countries to invite the Danish prime minister Anders Fogh Rasmussen to a meeting to discuss the matter. However, the prime minister refused to meet with the ambassadors, stating that a meeting would acknowledge that there was something to discuss. According to Rasmussen, there was nothing to discuss as Danish law protects freedom of the press. This led to a boycott of Danish products in Muslim countries, by which Arla was especially hard hit; in 2006, it was estimated to have lost over 400 million Danish crowns because of the boycott. In other words, one local event can rapidly evolve and spread across national borders.

Risks and crises

Risks and crises are inherently intertwined. Risks can be described as dangerous events that have a certain likelihood of occurring, and that can have serious consequences for an organization (Andersen & Spitzberg, 2009). Both natural factors, such as floods, thunderstorms and earthquakes, and human factors, such as wrong decisions or mistakes in, for example, nuclear power plants, lie behind risks. Crises can be viewed as a risk that has manifested or materialized (Heath & O'Hair, 2009). A risk turns into a crisis situation when the risk itself is not properly handled after it has arisen. Nevertheless, the mutual relationship between risk and crises has not been commonly discussed in the literature, though the research on risk and crises has developed in parallel in different disciplines. On an overall level, risk communication is characterized by information on any specific risk from an expert to a receiving group (Palenchar, 2009). The aim is thus to inform the recipients about the existence of a risk. It is expected that this information will give the recipients better knowledge and thus better capabilities to avoid potentially harmful risks. According to Heath and O'Hair (2009, p. 9), both risk and crisis communication are built on the cultural stereotype "You can't make an omelet without breaking an egg." In other words, no development is possible without a certain degree of risk-taking involved.

One problem with the concepts of risk and crisis is that they are rather vague terms, which can become problematic if they are used too broadly or without reflection. Already more than 50 years ago, Charles F. Hermann (1963) noted that crises are characterized by threats, surprise and quick response times. The challenge with crises is that we tend to be really surprised when they occur, and our typical explanatory models don't work in the situation (Carroll, 2015). Although there is no commonly accepted definition of an organizational crisis, Lerbinger's classic definition is considered commonplace. According to Lerbringer (1997, p. 4), an organizational crisis is "an event that brings, or has the potential for bringing, an organization into disrepute and imperils its future profitability, growth, and possibly its very survival."

In other words, an organizational crisis is a situation in which an organization is unable to continue with its normal operations. It is a common notion that a crisis is recognizable by the fact that it comes as a surprise, and that it comes without any warning signs; a crisis usually seems unimaginable at the time it occurs, but is still a predictable event (Heath & Millar, 2004). The American organizational psychologist Karl E. Weick (1988) describes a crisis as a low-probability situation with major consequences that threaten the most important and fundamental goals of an organization. A crisis often occurs unexpectedly, at an unlikely time. Crises can also be said to be threatening and to create an uncertain situation that requires a quick response time (Lerbringer, 2012). Crises thus threaten the normal order and create a great deal of insecurity in the organization, which must be managed (Falkheimer & Heide, 2010).

There are a number of different definitions for the word *crises*, but the one that we feel falls best in line with our view of crises comes from the crisis communications researchers Ulmer, Sellnow and Seeger (see the following box).

Definition of crisis

An organizational crisis is a specific, *unexpected* and *nonroutine* event or series of events that create high levels of *uncertainty* and *threaten* or are perceived to threaten an organization's *high-priority goals*.

– Ulmer, Sellnow, and Seeger (2007, p. 7)

Organizational crises often injure or endanger a stakeholder group, and thus can deteriorate the relationship with these stakeholders. Furthermore, a common consequence of organizational crises is that the legitimacy of the organization and the confidence that various stakeholders have in that organization is severely damaged. Modern research literature emphasizes that crises are perceptions of events rather than the events themselves, which means that what is perceived to be a crisis differs from person to person. Consequentially, there are many different perceptions of what constitutes a crisis for an organiza-tion. In many cases, management, co-workers, journalists, politicians, consumers and suppliers all have different views about *when* and *why* an organizational crisis occurs.

W. Timothy Coombs (2019), one of the world's leading crisis com-munications researchers, emphasizes that stakeholders' perceptions determine whether or not a situation is an organizational crisis.

> If people perceive there to be an organizational crisis, then there is a crisis, and people will respond to the organization as if it were in a crisis.
>
> – Coombs (2019, p. 3)

This implies that if co-workers perceive there to be an organizational crisis, then a smart management team would take this into consid-eration and act appropriately to avoid worsening the situation and creating a crisis of confidence against them. Several researchers (e.g., Olaniran, 2007; Penrose, 2000) argue that the perception of a crisis affects the consequences and results of the crisis. Although crises are most commonly viewed in a negative light, they can be greatly positive if organizational members can find the positive in a crisis situation and focus on opportunities for development. This could involve changing the organization's values, operations and leadership philosophy.

> When people believe there is a crisis, they are likely to behave differently than they would in so-called normal times.
>
> – Sellnow and Seeger (2013, p. 5)

Organizational crises are often a consequence of an incident inside or outside of the organization, though it is possible that a *double crisis* may occur due to poor management of or a lack of communication during a crisis (Frandsen & Johansen, 2017). For example, an awkward or insensitive maneuver from the CEO or another organizational actor can lead to a *trust crisis* for the organization, which may ultimately take many years and require huge amounts of commitment and work to recover from. Sohn and Lariscy (2014, p. 24) define a trust crisis as "[a] major event that has the potential to threaten collective perceptions and estimations held by all relevant stakeholders of an organization and its relevant attributes." According to Palm and Falkheimer (2005, p. 26), an organization has a trust crisis when "enough influential target groups and stakeholders have lost ample confidence" (our translation) They divide trust crises into two categories:

- Moral trust crises
- Competency trust crises

The former can stem from, for example, concerns about organizational leaders who go on luxury vacations and claim undue benefits on company costs. The latter crisis can be in respect to the competency levels of organizational leaders and members, for example, in response to market and environmental changes, which can have major negative consequences for the organization.

Why do crises occur?

The debate and conversation surrounding why crises occur have been very intense. The conversation can be grouped into three categories:

- Normal mistakes and interactional complexity
- Deficiencies in warning systems, risk perception and foresight
- Collapse of vigilance (Sellnow & Seeger, 2013)

The first category, *normal mistakes and interactional complexity*, is related to the crises that occur as a result of mistakes in the large complex systems of which organizations consist. In an increasingly complex society, the risk of crises is also increasing. The American sociology professor Charles Perrow (1984) claims that serious incidents are more or less impossible to avoid, regardless of how much organizations try to avoid them. This applies especially to complex high-risk organizations, such as chemical industries, nuclear power plants and other process industries. Perrow's *normal accident theory* (NAT) explains that the complexity of large, advanced sociotechnical systems, in which the different parts of the system are closely linked to each other, can very easily become vulnerable. These systems are usually so closely interconnected that one mistake in any part of the system has can have major and severe consequences for the other parts of the system. In addition, the system typically doesn't have enough slack in it, which means that decision-makers have no warning time before the entire system is affected. History has shown that many of the major natural disasters (e.g., floods, landslides and earthquakes) are often linked to complex built systems, such as dams and residential areas (Sellnow & Seeger, 2013).

The second category, *deficiencies in warning systems, risk perception and foresight*, describes the occurrence of crises due to risks that are either unpredicted or underestimated. Organizational members often do not understand and interpret the risks properly or, alternatively, do not succeed in communicating these risks up to management (see Chapter 5). For example, at the hospital we studied for this book, the system for managing deviations did not work optimally. The law states that all deviations from the normal, so, for example, when a patient is injured or nearly injured, must be reported. These reports are first taken care of locally by a manager or a quality control coordinator. In more serious cases, or when several deviations of the same nature have occurred, they are reported to the clinic's management team. In our interviews with nurses in the department, we found that although reports should be written every day, it often does not happen because of stress and a time shortage. In other words, there are warning system shortages in the hospital. Furthermore, co-workers can differently interpret what a risk is. The shortcomings of this warning system could consequently lead to an organizational crisis.

The third category, *collapse of vigilance*, can be accredited to Janis (1982), who is known for his theory on groupthink. Groupthink is a risk that arises after a group of people have worked together for a long time and thus develop a similar way of perceiving and valuing things together. Groupthink means that members of a group seek consistency and consensus in their decisions. Consequentially, the group becomes critical of information that does not conform to their own perspectives, making it difficult for individual team members to present alternative views. It is therefore easier for group members to remain quiet rather than challenge the status quo and consensus when making decisions. Another consequence of groupthink is that the ability to critically assess information and risks deteriorates (Sellnow & Seeger, 2013). One example of a crisis that arose as a result of groupthink is the *Challenger* disaster of 1986.

Challenger disaster

The *Challenger* disaster occurred in January 1986, when an explosive fire started aboard the US space shuttle during its launch from the Kennedy Space Center. All seven of the crew onboard died – some had survived the initial explosion but died from the impact of the space shuttle against the ocean. The explosion occurred because a seal, called an O-ring, was not sufficiently elastic for the cold weather on the day of takeoff. The O-ring should have stopped leakage of the hot gases that formed during launch, but due to its failure, the gas leaked and burned holes on the external fuel tank used at the start, and 700 tons of fluxing oxygen and hydrogen ignited and created an explosion. Technicians at NASA had long noted the shortcomings of the O-rings packing capability in cold weather. Nevertheless, they chose to ignore this information, as they felt pressured to produce results and keen to launch the spacecraft. The decision of management to launch the aircraft can most likely be explained in part by groupthink. Members of management refused to believe the information from technicians as this would have hindered launch of the *Challenger*.

Crisis management

Interest in crisis management has increased greatly amongst companies, consultants and researchers, following Johnson & Johnson's attempt to restore legitimacy after the 1982 Tylenol crisis, when a production worker managed to add cyanide to the popular Tylenol pills. As a result, seven people who ate the tablets died. The unknown production worker added 65 milligrams of cyanide into the Tylenol capsules, which is 10,000 times more than is needed to kill a person. This crisis put fear into many business executives, and consultants struck gold by encouraging them to see potential risks and crises everywhere and urging them to be prepared for all possible situations, which usually caused them to realize that they were not sufficiently prepared to handle these crises (Heath & O'Hair, 2009). *Crisis management* has two overall objectives:

- *Prevent* a crisis from taking place
- *Alleviate* the effects of a crisis that has occurred

Crises are often said to be preceded by different warning signals, and one of the main objectives of crisis management is to detect these signals. It is not, however, always so simple, which will be discussed in more detail in the forthcoming chapters. Hindsight is 20/20, and it is much easier to say that you should have acted one way or another in the aftermath of an event than to actually have the foresight to actually do so. Here, co-workers have an important role to play, as they have the best expertise and longest experience of specific work tasks in the organization. Managers and management also have an important role as they can see other, more comprehensive signals of a possible imminent crisis. The French crisis researcher Patrick Lagadec (1993) emphasizes that an organization's ability to cope with a crisis largely correlates with the *structure that was developed before* confusion and chaos arose, and research has shown that organizations with a rigid structure and hierarchy are particularly sensitive to mistakes.

Overconfidence in crisis plans

Even today, strong emphasis is placed on the importance of crisis planning and a crisis communication plan. Coombs (2006) states that too many organizational leaders believe that the existence of a crisis plan is the same as crisis management. Much of the research has also been devoted to studying and evaluating such plans, and researchers pose the question, "Do you have a crisis plan?" to organizations. These plans are seen as the main tool for dealing with a crisis. Some researchers like Fearn-Banks (2016) see crisis plans as a "collective brain" that organizational members can use in times of crisis when there is great uncertainty and confusion. However, crisis plans are just a tool and therefore not a final goal in and of themselves.

Important *processes* are involved in planning and working with crisis plans, which are an important part of improving the preparations before the discovery and management of a crisis. However, the work does not end once a crisis plan is produced and decided upon; once the plan has been created, it is important to start the heavy lifting on implementing the crisis plan in the organization and to create a general *crisis awareness* within the organization, wherein leadership is fundamentally important and repeated crisis exercises are continually carried out for skill strengthening. Marra (1998, 2004) emphasizes that it is not the crisis plan per se that determines whether crisis preparedness and crisis management are excellent but, instead, that *organizational culture* and the exercising of *leadership* play a large role.

Recently, there has been criticism of excessive confidence in crisis and crisis communication plans and the amount of energy that is spent developing the "optimal" Plan (with a capital *P*). The over-exaggerated confidence that we can have in crisis plans is based on the belief that organizations can be completely rational and have the ability to predict all possible crisis scenarios. The problem with crisis plans is that they

- can give an unwarranted feeling of safety,
- can delay organizations' reaction times and decision-making processes and
- are rarely updated and are thus riddled with irrelevant information (Falkheimer et al., 2009).

Marra (2004) goes so far as to say that organizations with crisis plans actually manage crises worse than those that do not have plans in place. Although this can be considered an overexaggeration, there is a risk that organizations place too much energy on *formulating* crisis plans and not enough on implementing the plans in an organization and working to develop crisis awareness. This is to say that the value of a crisis plan lies in its ability to be a mental support for organization members in the initial phase of a crisis – an aid in initiating the first and most important measure of crisis management. Once the initial stages are initiated, the wise organization switches to improvisation, as each crisis situation is unique, and the appropriate measure must be determined on a situational basis.

When conducting our study at the university hospital, both the communications strategy and the communications plan for crisis situations were lacking. When the university hospital was originally created, the two existing crisis plans from Lund University Hospital and Malmö University Hospital were still in place. It was clear in this situation that the communications manager had no deeper knowledge of these plans, which is understandable given that they covered 150 pages each. The communications manager explained that

> [t]he preparedness of the communication department is based on our previous experiences. We cannot rely on the documents [the crisis plans] – that would drive us crazy!
> (Heide & Simonsson, 2014a, p. 137)

The problem for the university hospital at the time was partly that they had two different crisis plans in place, which were extremely comprehensive and detailed, though based on different experiences and traditions and thus not unified. This means that, in practice, they did not have any practical significance for the event of a crisis, and the risk was that the plans were more of a hindrance than a help during an emergency.

Phases of a crisis and previous research in crisis communication

In both research and in practice, organizational crises are typically divided up into different phases. This makes it easier to describe and understand a crisis process, as well as to analyze and determine how it should be managed in the different phases. In reality, there is no determined beginning and end to a crisis, but creating a division between phases of a crisis has an education and practical value. The literature on *crisis management* has different models for the division of a crisis. Fink (1986) offers a four-step model, whereas Mitroff (1994) instead chooses to divide the course into five phases. Turner's (1976) model has six stages. However, it is most common, and perhaps easiest, to divide the crisis into three phases (see Figure 1.3). Meyers (1987) denotes these stages as pre-crisis, crisis and post-crisis.

In the *pre-crisis* phase, organizations need to focus on noticing warning signals of an impending crisis. These can be quick or slow changes, and different incident or accidents. Crises are, as mentioned earlier, most often a result of different risk factors either going unnoticed or being discovered too late. Noticing risk factors is a complex

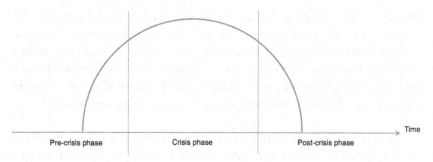

Figure 1.3 Phases of a crisis

process that requires both taking in information from different sources and interpreting them correctly. For this to happen, an organization needs to have an open and supportive communications climate, wherein leadership promotes and rewards the reporting of negative information.

> Missed warnings, flawed communication about a perceived threat, failed interpretations and/or failure to act upon warnings, then, are typically associated with the development of a crisis.
> – Sellnow and Seeger (2013, p. 50)

The *crisis phase* begins after someone has decided that the organization is in crisis and that action needs to be taken to quickly correct and manage the situation. In this case, many organizations activate a crisis team whose task is to assess the situation and take the first steps. Crisis teams can comprise of, for example, the CEO, the chief of security and the communications manager. Many times, there is also a media center with enhanced telephone services and staff responsible for answering questions and following channels in different social media.

During the acute phase of a crisis, it is important to inform interested parties and journalists as fast as possible, so that they can spread the information with the public. In the post-crisis phase, it is important for the organization to recover by undertaking activities that will help to get back their public trust, image and legitimacy, as well as to undergo a learning process to minimize the risk that a similar crisis situation will occur again.

Most of the research on crisis communication has focused on the acute crisis phase, and how organizations can reestablish their reputation after a crisis has occurred. Crises are perceived as isolated and clearly delimited events, which require a quick and direct response. External communications and reactive *damage control* lie at the vortex of this communication, that is, trying to reduce and prevent the negative consequences of the crisis (Kent, 2010). The research has been characterized by a strong focus on crisis management plans: excellent plans are considered the key to success for crisis management, and overconfidence is often placed in the importance of information. During this phase, communications are often reduced to simply spreading information to different target groups, carefully forming press releases, having contact lists for journalists, and educating spokespersons (Gilpin & Murphy, 2008). All these communications are expected to deliver the same message and in the same form to all potential stakeholders and recipients. The hope is that the cleverly planned and implemented communications processes will alleviate the effects of a crisis and thus restore the organization's reputation and image.

At the center of much previous research in crisis communication is how organizations repair their image. One of the first research papers on crises from a communications perspective is "They spoke in defense of themselves" (Ware & Linkugel, 1973). In this paper, the authors discuss different strategies for defending reputations. They identified four different types of strategies:

- Denial: I didn't do it.
- Bolstering: I'm a nice person. I can't have done it.
- Differentiation: Distancing oneself.
- Transcendence: A higher purpose.

Much of the early research in crisis communication was conducted by rhetoricians, and they focused, in particular, on defense and persuasion after a crisis. Within the field of strategic communication, research scientist William Benoit (1997) created *image restoration theory*, which is one of the most well-known theories within crisis communications and describes a model for the restoration of the organizational image after a crisis. This theory builds on *apologia* (rhetorical defense strategies), and Benoit has identified five approaches:

- Denial
- Evading responsibility
- Reducing offensiveness
- Corrective action
- Mortification

Public relations researcher Timothy Coombs (2019) has further developed Benoit's theory, which only offers a limited number of crisis defense strategies, and has created *Situational Crisis Communication Theory* (SCCT). This theory is based on attribution theory, which explains that people are constantly trying to find causes – attributes – to negative events. Individuals then react emotionally (disappointment, anger, contempt) based on the attributes that they have ascribed to the situation. The starting point for SCCT is that organizations must first assess the type of threat and the risk it poses based on three factors: initial crisis responsibility, crisis history and prior relational reputation. From there, SCCT offers 11 different defense strategies that are grouped into four main categories:

- Denial
- Diminishment
- Rebuilding
- Bolstering

Both *image restoration theory* and SCCT focus on strategies that organizations can use after a crisis has happened (post-crisis).

The traditional research on crisis communication has gained increasing criticism in recent years – not least for its one-sided emphasis on the acute phase, a simplified, asymmetric view of communications and overconfidence in control and planning capabilities. In the wake of this criticism, alternative perspectives have emerged, including Gilpin and Murphy's (2008) complexity theory. This theory stands in contrast to traditional and linear crisis communication models that tend to reduce complexity in a crisis. Instead, complexity theory is based on a social constructionist perspective, which means that individuals' interpretations are crucial to their understanding and actions.

This theory emphasizes that it is not possible to predict and plan in a rational way but that, instead, proactivity and on-the-spot improvisation are the keys to success in crisis management.

In the next chapter we go into the traditional versus new, alternative perspectives in further depth. The alternative approaches also more strongly emphasize the internal aspects of crisis communications.

Chapter 2

Perspectives on crises and crisis communication

RESEARCH IS NEITHER neutral nor objective but is instead based on different theoretical viewpoints that color the choice of research questions, objects of study and the ultimate analysis and interpretation. Though the underlying viewpoints in research are not always explicitly expressed, they often have a large effect on the results generated by the research. Likewise, in organizations' practical work on crisis management, it is possible to discern underlying norms and values that characterize the organization's perception of what constitutes a crisis and how to decide the best course of crisis management.

In this chapter, we discuss two overall perspectives and visualize what they mean for our understanding and knowledge of crises. We first discuss these two perspectives from a research point of view, and then we give examples of how these perspectives are reflected in practice.

Perspectives in research

As we have already discussed, most research on crisis communications is closely related to public relation research. The research on public relations has traditionally been grounded in a functionalist perspective with an emphasis on rationality, control and predictability (Holtzhausen, 2012). As it is primarily public relations researchers who have studied crisis communications, the same rationalistic thinking also dominates this field.

In recent years, an alternative approach has developed, which has been our starting point in our research and writing for this book. This approach goes by several different names, such as late modern crisis communication (Falkheimer & Heide, 2010), postmodern perspective (Tyler, 2005) and complexity theory (Gilpin & Murphy, 2010). These perspectives are unified in their philosophical basis, that is to say, in how to approach and understand knowledge. Each of these theories is based on social constructionism, which views individuals' understanding of reality as socially constructed, meaning that we understand and act based on our own understanding of different phenomena. We all have different understandings of, for example, an organization. This understanding is built on, among other things, our own experiences, interests and education. We do not build this understanding entirely on our own but, instead, to a large extent it is constructed in communication with other people. This means that more than one social reality can exist within an organization and that there is often one strong and dominant story within an organization, such as what it prioritizes and values.

The social constructionist approach goes hand in hand with the idea that a crisis is a perception (see Chapter 1, page 17). In many ways, it is also a much broader approach than the functionalist perspective – not least in terms of the sorts of crises that are studied, which parts of the crises are emphasized and the sorts of communicative processes that are of interest. Advocates of this alternative approach turn away from the classical broadcast orientation of research – the transfer of information from experts to "common" people. Instead, they emphasize communication as a process of sensemaking, with an interactive approach between institutions/organizations and different groups.

The traditional, functionalist perspective and the alternative social constructionist perspective both go, as mentioned earlier, under different terms. For simplicity, we will use the following terms when discussing the two perspectives (cf. Frandsen & Johansen, 2017):

• The narrow, information-oriented approach
• The broad, meaning-oriented approach

The narrow, information-oriented approach

In line with a functionalist perspective, much of the traditional research has focused on finding generalizable results that can help organizations become more effective in their crisis management. The wishes of practitioners that researchers identify "best practices" can also be seen as an expression of a belief in generalizable, prescriptive knowledge. Within this narrow view of crises, there are also a lot of pieces of advice and checklists for practitioners regarding how they should react in a crisis situation in order to handle it as effectively as possible. One classic piece of advice is "tell everything, tell it quickly, and tell the whole truth." This advice rarely works in practice, as there are many different understandings of what constitutes the "truth" (Tyler, 2005). It should probably be pointed out here that we are in no way against good examples or good advice. We are, however, skeptical about good examples that are presented as universal models, applicable to all types of organizations and crisis situations, or good advice that presumes simple truths.

Regarding the various phases of a crisis, the narrow perspective has focused primarily on the acute phase, that is, the period just after the crisis has begun (Heath, 2010). As a consequence, researchers have largely studied fairly reactive communications activities – "damage control" and "image repair" – rather than proactive activities, emphasizing how to prevent and capture weak signals on what can turn into a crisis (see Chapter 1). The purpose of crisis research is to help organizations to mitigate the impact of the crisis and to return to the status quo as quickly and efficiently as possible. The strong emphasis on control and simple models reflects a traditional view of rationality, where management and other managers are presumed to have the best requisites for making informed decisions. Deetz (1992) writes about "managerialism," which is a concept that easily fits into the context. Managerialism can be seen as a discourse that is driven by the idea that the organization can be equated with the management and bosses; the organization and its leaders are an entity separate from the other co-workers and stakeholders. The main purpose of managerialism is control, and it is driven by instrumental, economic motivations.

The narrow perspective is also related to the view of crises as a result of external forces, something that suddenly comes from outside, requiring immediate response and management vis-à-vis external groups and stakeholders (Gilpin & Murphy, 2008). The view of crises as something that comes from outside can also be seen as an explanation of why the internal perspective and internal communication have been neglected in the traditional research perspective. Crises are further regarded as quite distinct events with a clear beginning and a definite end (Rosenthal, Boin, & Comfort, 2001). A crisis is thus seen as a spatially and temporally delimited phenomenon, and it is not uncommon that a scapegoat that "caused" the crisis is searched for.

When considering how communication is viewed, the narrow approach is related to a simplified view of communication, the so-called transmission view, which emphasizes the transmission of information between a sender and a receiver, and assumes that words contain more or less definite meanings that the recipient can decode and take in (Carey, 2009). The problem with this viewpoint is that it gives the illusion that communication is a fairly simple, linear process wherein the channels/media and words are central. Communication is furthermore considered to be a tool; cleverly planned and well-implemented communication is believed to mitigate the effects of the crisis and restore the organization's image. Kent (2010) is critical of this approach and believes that too much of the crisis research has been based on the organization's or company's perspective and that more research is needed from the perspective of "crisis-afflicted" and other interested parties.

The broad, meaning-oriented approach

Advocates of the broad approach emphasize the complexity that pervades many of today's organizations. Gilpin and Murphy (2010) state that "crisis managers need to develop a tolerance for looser quality, lighter controls, and limited predictability" (p. 685). Routine actions and predetermined plans can work in stable situations, but each crisis situation is unique and thus requires the ability to improvise and act on the basis of the current situation. However, although improvisation relies on flexibility and customization, it is not an entirely random and spontaneous process. Weick (1998) claims that improvisation requires both solid experience and what he called a steady beat that can be a platform for more advanced composition in the actual situation. More concretely put, a "steady beat" can be a simple crisis management plan that serves as an overall framework rather than a detailed manual. The broad approach does therefore not reject the value of crisis management plans but, instead, ensures that we do not exaggerate the importance of these plans.

In line with the idea of organizational complexity, crises are regarded as procedural and integrated phenomena instead of distinct, isolated events with a clear beginning and end. Taking inspiration from chaos theory, crises are usually seen as a result of a number of minor, reciprocal events, which are often in turn related to complex, systemic occurrences instead of being solitary events or individuals (Bechler, 2004; Kersten, 2005). This perception of crises as dynamic and processional also emphasizes all the three phases of a crisis and the relationship between them.

This approach is not only broader in the sense that all the phases of a crisis are studied, but also in the sense that it takes on a broader view of what constitutes a crisis. In this approach, crises are perceived as perceptual phenomena, as socially constructed (see Chapter 1), and are thus defined in terms of human interpretations and actions rather than "actual" course of events. The broad perceptual approach opens the study of more "everyday" occurrences, such as a company merger or termination of co-workers, as a crisis. This also means that crises affect not only organizations and their management but also co-workers and other stakeholders (Kent, 2010).

The perceptual view of crisis is closely linked to a meaning perspective on communication – an emphasis on the complexity of communication and the meaning that arises in the interactions between people. Several researchers emphasize that crisis situations are often characterized by confusion, ambiguity and an experience of disorientation. Weick (1993) claims that a *cosmology episode* often occurs in connection with crises:

> [W]hen people suddenly and deeply feel that the universe is no longer a rational, orderly system. What makes such an episode so shattering is that both the sense of what is occurring and the means to rebuild that sense collapse together.
>
> (p. 633)

A turbulent situation involves a deviation from the normal, stable situation, wherein the usual interpretive frames are put out of play, which, in turn, "triggers" a process of active sensemaking. When we are in a crisis, we have a great need for communication, both in terms of "simple" directives on how to protect ourselves and in terms of more complex information about the causes, implications and consequences that help us to interpret the situation. We try to create understandings of what happens, how serious it is, what it means and what we should do (Weick & Sutcliffe, 2003). This approach clarifies that there are many different interpretations of a (crisis) situation (Ulmer, Sellnow, & Seeger, 2011). This means that there are many different perceptions among co-workers, depending on the profession, knowledge, network, hierarchical position and experience.

The broad, meaning-oriented approach highlights the importance of a continuous and symmetrical relationship between the organization and its stakeholders. Wan and Pfau (2004) pointed out the importance

Table 2.1 A comparison between the narrow, information-oriented and the broad, meaning-oriented approaches.

	Narrow approach	Broad approach
View of crises	Objective events with a certain meaning	Crises are a social construction – perception
Crisis phase in focus	Acute crisis phase	All crises phases
Research interest	Find general, "rule of thumb" results	Increase the understanding of crises as socially constructed
View of leadership	Managerialism, rationality – plans and checklists	Complexity and flexibility/ improvisation
View of communication	Transmission view	Sensemaking view
Relationship to stakeholders	Asymmetrical	Relational, symmetrical

of such an orientation early on and found that "vaccination" with positive messages about an organization improves the ability to cope with a crisis situation for all stakeholders. This vaccination is even more robust and resilient if the organization has managed to establish a good relationship with its main stakeholders.

The main differences between the two approaches can be found in Table 2.1.

As mentioned earlier, we advocate the broad, meaning-oriented approach – not least because it opens up for space for more strategic and long-term crisis management.

Approaches in practice

We have described and discussed two different approaches to crises and crisis communication above. These approaches are theoretical perspectives that permeate research, but we can also see links between these approaches and how to view and manage crises and crisis communication in practice. Our analysis of the university hospital's crisis management showed that it largely mirrored the narrow, information-oriented approach.

We develop this by explaining the situation the organization was in, how co-workers perceived the situation and what the formal crisis definition looked like.

The co-workers' perspective

As previously mentioned, the hospital we chose to study has undergone a major merger in recent years – a change that was quickly decided on, but the implementation of which has then been underway for several years and is still ongoing. The merger was debated and met with criticism, not least from the physicians. In parallel with the merger, the hospital has been under strict budget requirements, and at the same time, the legal requirements for patient safety have increased. In the wake of this, the media has reported on, among other things, co-workers who resign due to high stress levels, increased number of patient registrations, critique from internal auditors and critique from the Work Environment Authority. Media reports are, of course, based on the so-called media logic with an emphasis on the negative, dramatic and polarizing (Altheide & Snow, 1979), and one can debate how nuanced or impartial this media image actually is. This is the image of the hospital that patients, citizens, co-workers, politicians and other groups see in the media. There are also other signs that the hospital as an organization is strained. For example, one summer a number of weekly demonstrations were organized in which co-workers, medical students and other sympathizers protested against further cuts by lying on the ground outside the hospital center (as also reported in the regional news media). Begun a few years ago, an open group on Facebook named "Save the University Hospital" has had approximately 6,600 members (both co-workers and citizens). This group holds discussions about events and decisions related to the healthcare system – typically from a critical perspective.

All in all, a number of factors point toward the fact that the hospital as an organization has been in a tense and turbulent situation for a long time. But the question that remains is whether this can be considered a crisis situation. In our interviews with co-workers in the hospital, we asked how they viewed the concept of crisis and what sort of crisis they had encountered during their time at the hospital. The answers to these questions made it clear that some co-workers considered the current situation to be, in fact, a crisis:

> A crisis is when I am unable to fulfill my job duties, and this is happening more and more often nowadays.
>
> (Nurse)

> Right now, we are so short-staffed so that when a co-worker is sick and calls in to have someone cover them, you cannot find someone as everyone is too tired or won't answer the phone as they have already worked so much overtime. If people don't answer the phone because of our current job conditions, how will they be able to answer in the case of an emergency?
>
> (Doctor)

The preceding quotes signal that there are co-workers who feel that the organization as a whole is in crisis. The second quote comes from a doctor who indicated that the hospital has no good emergency preparedness in place. Some units have more or less constant staff shortages, and the doctor indicated that there are no reserves to deal with any future emerging crisis and the entailing consequences. The previously mentioned protests and co-workers referring to the news media to express their frustration and concern can also be seen as indications that some co-workers both perceive and act as if the organization is in a crisis.

The formal perspective on crisis

The co-workers' experiences of working in an organization in crisis can be compared with the view of crises expressed in the hospital's crisis management plan. This plan states that the third and final emergency level – disaster mode – is triggered when

> [a] situation where the available resources are insufficient in relation to the emergency care need, and where the load is so high that normal quality requirements for medical treatment cannot be sustained despite adequate measures.

This quote reflects a focus on care, resources and the acute phase of a crisis (even the two lower levels of preparedness emphasize the same factors). This emphasis on resources linked to the provision of care and the acute situation was also seen when we asked our interviewees about how they view a crisis. The crisis management plan gives some examples of events that may activate the emergency plan: fires, serious electrical malfunctions, bomb threats, water leaks, elevator problems and so on. The preceding quote, as well as examples of crises, goes hand in hand with the narrow, information-oriented approach to crises. In the next chapter we give more examples of how this approach is also reflected in ways of looking at and working with crisis communications. What we want to highlight here is that formal crisis preparedness is rather narrow in its view of crises and does not contain crises linked to, for example, leadership, working environment and trust. If we use the earlier definition of a crisis, it is difficult to claim that the hospital is in a crisis – even if there are reports of mistakes and a lack of patient safety that can be seen as a result of a poor working environment. However, this does not prevent co-workers from experiencing and, to some extent, acting as if the hospital is in a crisis.

In order to further clarify our reasoning, we have compiled a four-field typology of different types of crises based on two different parameters (please see Figure 2.1). The following are the two parameters:

- *Suddenly occurring versus slowly emerging crisis:* A suddenly occurring crisis leads to more or less immediate consequences and demands a rapid response from management and others in the organization. With slowly emerging, we mean crises that arise gradually over a long time. Emerging crises rarely require an immediate action but often take a long time to remedy and require comprehensive and systemic measures to be fixed.
- *External versus internal origin:* Where the crisis has arisen – outside or inside the organization (see Frandsen & Johansen, 2017).

According to our interpretation, the slowly developing crises – especially those of an internal origin and without a direct connection to medicine – are a blind spot in the formal hospital crisis management plan. Epidemics, which are at least in some cases slowly developed, do, however, have a clear connection to the medical perspective and are also a part of their formal crisis preparedness. To a great extent, problems related to the work environment, leadership and co-worker

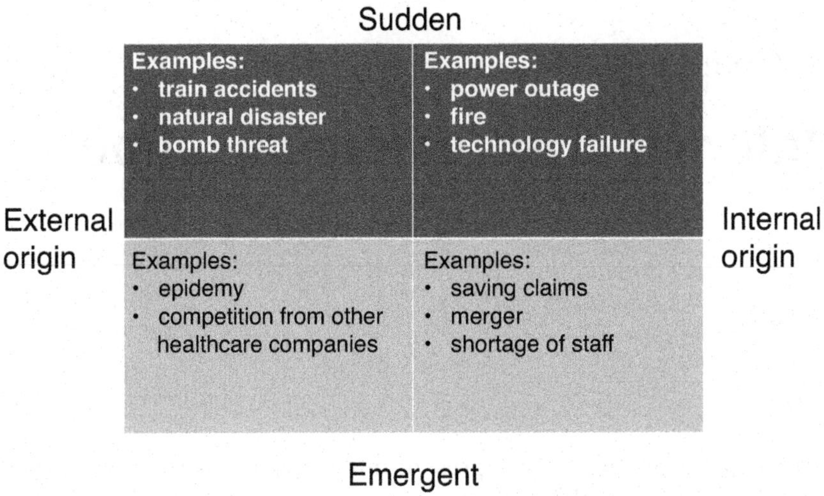

Sudden

Examples: • train accidents • natural disaster • bomb threat	**Examples:** • power outage • fire • technology failure
Examples: • epidemy • competition from other healthcare companies	Examples: • saving claims • merger • shortage of staff

External origin · · · Internal origin

Emergent

Figure 2.1 Different types of crises

confidence seem to be issues that are expected to be handled in the day-to-day work of management.

Our point is not that the management of all types of crises should be covered by a single crisis management plan. To the contrary, we think it would be valuable to take on a broader view of crises, which considers slowly emerging crises of an internal origin, and that can answer to how these crises look from an co-worker perspective. James and Wooten (2005) argue that almost three quarters of all organizational crises emerge slowly from an internal origin.

? Discussion

One common piece of advice is that all organizations should prepare for different types of crises, as all kinds of crises can occur in all kinds of organizations.

Use an organization that you have experience with and consider which types of crises the organization would be best prepared for and which it would not be aware of or prepared for.

Chapter 3

Internal crisis communication

IN THIS CHAPTER we first present our viewpoint on internal crisis communication. In the following sections we present an overview of previous research on internal crisis communications and subsequently discuss how communication with co-workers differs from communication with external individuals and groups. The final sections deal with the goals of internal crisis communication and the kinds of communication that should be prioritized during the various phases of the crisis.

What is internal crisis communication?

Internal crisis communication may seem like a self-explanatory concept. A basic definition is that it entails *the communication that occurs with an organization in connection to a crisis.* At the same time, there are a number of aspects of this simple definition that can be discussed.

First off, it is not always easy to delineate an organization's boundaries and to distinguish between what is *internal and external* communications. Organizations are increasingly porous – not least due to social media, which blurs the lines between internal and external communications. If a group of co-workers starts a Facebook group that is open for the public and then discusses topics about their employer in this group, is this internal or external communication? Different types of organizational forms and employment relationships have also blurred the borders between internal and external. Take the example of temp workers: consultants and personnel hired from external agencies are external bodies that can play an important role in the organization's internal communications (Heide, Johansson, & Simonsson, 2012). This can also be seen during crises, which are typically complex and rarely take place solely within the borders of one organization (Gilpin & Murphy, 2008). Major crises such as powerful floods, epidemics, or terrorist attacks often require close work between several different organizations (hospitals, police, firefighters, state bureaus, etc.), which goes to show just how unclear the limits of internal communications can be.

Second, the meaning of "*in connection to*" is not self-evident. As we previously mentioned, most previous research has focused solely on what happens during the most acute phase of a crisis. Similar to many other researchers we would like to take a process-oriented perspective on crises – what happens during the critical phase is actually in the shadows of the pre- and post-crisis events ('t Hart, Heyse, & Boin, 2001). It is therefore important that crisis communication starts before the crisis actually begins; organizations need to conduct exercises and develop plans for how they will effectively communicate when faced with a crisis. It is of equal importance that organizations create a climate of open communication, wherein their co-workers feel comfortable taking accountability for their mistakes and where there are managers and assigned bodies in place that can recognize any so-called weak signals (Coombs, 2019) of what can develop into a crisis. Directly following a crisis, organizations tend to focus on managing their reputation. If not before, stakeholders will then question who was responsible and potentially lose faith in the organization's capabilities. At the same time, this phase offers organizations a great learning opportunity concerning how they can better prepare themselves for the next potential crisis. Crisis communication is therefore the communication that occurs before, during and after a crisis. It is not a one-time occurrence but is, instead, a continuous, long-term process with varying levels of intensity.

A third facet of crisis communication to consider is what is actually meant by the term *communication*. In the previous chapter we discussed various approaches to communication, and in this book, we have chosen to use a sensemaking perspective. Although the ability to communicate quickly and accurately during a crisis is crucial to effective crisis management, our focus in this book is not on fast channels or the transmission of information (Zimmerman, 2013). Instead, we have chosen to focus on the connection that communication has to culture, leadership, followership, learning and other organizational processes. Most of the previous research in this area has focused on what should be communicated during the acute phase of a crisis (Gilpin & Murphy, 2008). We will move away from this tactical focus and instead contribute with an understanding of how crises can be handled with a more long-term, strategic perspective. Moreover, we do not see communication as an isolated process, but instead, we want to emphasize the close connection that communication has to crisis management in general; we would like to highlight a communicative mindset that permeates all activities at all the levels of an organization.

In light of the preceding reasoning and with inspiration from Johansen et al. (2012), we define *internal crisis communication* as follows:

Definition of *internal crisis communication*

Internal crisis communication is the continuous communicative processes that take place between managers and co-workers and co-workers and co-workers before, during and after an organizational crisis.

Previous research on internal crisis communication – an overview

As we previously mentioned, research on crisis communication has for the most part been interested in how organizations handle communication with the media and other external bodies. Within the broader research area of *crisis management*, internal facets such as decision-making, learning and organizational culture have been studied but not with communication as the primary focus. While aspects of communication have been taken up and discussed, this has rarely been done explicitly or with communication as the clear analytical lens (e.g., Turner, 1994). This does not mean that crisis management research is irrelevant for developing an understanding of internal crisis communication, but we do need more research with a sharp focus on communication.

In this book, we will continuously refer to the relevant previous research that helps build an understanding of organizations' crisis communication. However, in this section we would like to give a brief overview of the previous research in this area. Although there are not that many publications focusing explicitly on internal crisis communication, it is hard to provide a complete overview, and we focus on the publications we have found most relevant.

The American professor in organization psychology Karl E. Weick's theory on sensemaking is greatly significant for the area of internal crisis communication. He has conducted a number of studies on how we make sense and understanding in crisis situations and the significance that this sensemaking holds for our behavior (Weick, 1988, 1990, 1993, 2010). Weick and Sutcliffe (2001, 2007) also make an interesting distinction between *anticipation*, or preparations before a crisis breaks out (such as uncovering mistakes and creating contingency plans), and *resilience*, which refers to an organization's learning and recovery capabilities after a crisis. These concepts are discussed in Chapters 5 and 6. Weick is also one of the foreground figures behind the theory of High Reliability Organization (HRO), which is another of the theoretical pillars of this book (see Chapter 5, page 81).

Although Weick's theories are highly pertinent to our understanding of internal crisis communication, they are more based on an organizational psychological perspective than a communicative perspective. However, a number of studies that clearly focus on communication have been published during the past few years. One such publication came from the Danish crisis communication researchers Finn Frandsen and Winni Johansen (2011), in which they created a framework for future studies of internal crisis communication. They discuss the concept of internal stakeholders, such as managers and co-workers, and how they differ from other types of stakeholders in relation to a crisis, as developed in the next section of this chapter. The authors also make a breakdown of the different areas of internal crisis communication linked to the different phases of the crisis; these can serve as a good starting point for the student writing an essay or the practitioner reflecting on his or her work in the field.

In their article "Entering New Territory: A Study of Internal Crisis Management and Crisis Communication in Organizations," Johansen et al. (2012) present the results from a survey of 450 private and public organizations in Denmark. The point of the survey was to further uncover how organizations perceive, plan, coordinate and implement different crisis management and communication-oriented activities. The survey was directed at the personnel responsible for crisis management, which means that the study is more based on "expert opinion" than on how co-workers, in general, perceive internal crisis communication. The study presents several different interesting factors, such as perceptions of how co-workers react to crises, which communication channels are used and how common it is to have a crisis plan, a crisis communications policy, a designated manager for crisis management and so on. The results of this study show that most organizations have a relatively formal and professional crisis preparedness but that their plans and documents are more developed for external than for internal crisis management. There is also a strong correlation between an organization's size and its crisis management: the bigger the organization, the greater the chance is that they have a formal crisis management plan.

A third article in this area, written by Alessandra Mazzei and Silvia Ravazzani (2011), studied how effective internal communication was in Italian companies in relation to the global financial crisis in 2008–2009. The study is based both on interviews with co-workers and managers and on a survey of internal communication managers. The results show the importance of creating a trusting relationship between managers and co-workers *before* a crisis begins, often through active listening. If co-workers sense that managers are not listening to them, then there is a possibility that they will feel both abandoned and excluded, and at the same time, their knowledge will never be put to use.

Another article published by Mazzei and Ravazzani (2015) focused on Italian companies during the global financial crisis. The study was based on surveys of internal communications chiefs in 61 different companies. The purpose of this study was to examine different strategies for internal crisis communication, and the characteristics of that communication. The authors identify five different strategies and discuss them in relation to the need to maintain confidence and reputation in times of crisis. The results of the study show that these organizations are unaware of the importance of internal communication during crises and that the majority of the companies practice what the authors call "underuse" and "avoidance."

Mazzei, Kim and Dell'Oro (2012) have further developed the relationship between continuous, everyday communication and internal communication once the crisis has occurred. The authors conducted a case study of an Italian company where one co-worker had died in a workplace accident. The study analyzed different types of internal documents, such as web pages, policies and internal campaigns on workplace safety, and interviewed the manager in charge of internal communication on different occasions. This study illustrates that internal relationships, developed through both years of investment in co-worker safety and effective internal communication, are crucial for how co-workers communicate during a crisis. When co-workers are proud of and believe in their employers, they tend to act as ambassadors for the organization, and they subsequently do not directly place blame for the crisis on company leadership.

Strandberg and Vigsø (2016) have conducted a case study where they study not only the communication from the management to the co-workers but also the co-workers' communication with each other. The study was based on interviews with both managers and co-workers at a municipality where a former co-worker had been accused of financial fraud. While management blamed the former co-worker as the reason for the crisis, the co-workers felt that cultural problems were the main reason and that it was a shared responsibility. Some managers thought that they had handled the crisis quite well, but the co-workers did not agree on that. The co-workers thought that not all information was presented, which made them construct their own narratives based on rumors and their own assumptions. Strandberg and Vigsø (2016, p. 90) emphasize that "to be successful in internal crisis communication, managers need to be aware of the culture in the organization, and to be able to improvise, listen to the co-workers, and their need of sensemaking."

Korn and Einwiller (2013) have written an article that studies how critical media coverage of an organization can influence the co-workers. Negative media coverage is often problematic and even more problematic if not commented on by management. Korn and Einwiller mean that fast and transparent internal communication is helpful after the media have reported on an issue. If the internal communication works well, it can reduce co-workers need to look for more news in the media, and it can make them more comfortable in handling external stakeholders' reactions. Korn and Einwiller also found that colleagues are both an important information source and support during a crisis. Hence, it is important to emphasize and to constantly develop the internal communication in an organization for various reasons. A study by Zaumane (2016) shows even that inefficient internal communication in itself can lead to an organizational crisis.

Ravazzani (2016) has studied managers' perspectives on and practices of internal crisis communication in organizations with a multicultural environment. Although multicultural issues are part of most crises today, crisis communication research lack a cultural contextualization, especially regarding internal aspects of crisis communication. Ravazzani's interviews with Danish managers indicated that the cultural background of co-workers is perceived as particularly relevant when there is a geographical distance, that is, when co-workers are located in different countries. In those cases, managers rely very much on local leaders and communicators who act as cultural interpreters.

We have ourselves published three international articles on internal crisis communication, based on the same research project that we work off in this book (see Chapter 8, page 136) for a description of our methods and empirical materials. The first article (Heide & Simonsson, 2014a) presents an analysis of communicators' roles and practices in relation to the internal aspects of crisis communication. One result we found is that the communicators at the hospital we studied had a limited role regarding internal crisis communication. Their role involved for the most part spreading information via intranet, though there were examples where the communications function also involved strategic work during the acute phase of a crisis. The standard practice was that communicators were first called in after the crisis had already begun – a sort of *communication on demand* – which clearly limited the possibilities for strategic and long-term communications work. In the article, we give suggestions for and discuss new possible roles in relation to all the phases of a crisis.

In our second article (Heide & Simonsson, 2015), we try to challenge what we in the previous chapter called a narrow information-oriented view on crises. The purpose of the article is to highlight the complexity of internal crisis communication by analyzing a number of paradoxical tension fields we identified in the hospital study. Five tensions were discussed: episodic versus emergent, centralized versus decentralized, professional versus organizational, planning versus improvisation and external versus internal. Internal crisis communication is a complex phenomenon that demands a both-perspective rather than a simplistic either-or thinking. For example, it is important that we do not work solely with planning but that we also leave room for improvisation. We did, however, find a tendency by professionals to polarize toward one of the two ends of the mentioned fields of tension. At the end of the article we discuss the different ways to handle tensions and, among other things, we address the importance of meta-communication in creating a wider and more reflexive approach to crisis management.

In the third article (Simonsson & Heide, 2018) the aim is to produce new knowledge of how organizational errors can be used to early detect weak signals of changes that could develop into a crisis. A prerequisite is then a crisis awareness culture that is supported by a crisis leadership. A crisis awareness culture entails an understanding of mistakes as occasions for learning and an organizational ability to early capture weak signals of upcoming crises. Such a culture makes co-worker comfort to report on errors, and it is then possible to internally discuss and reflect on risks, mistake and near-mistakes that have occurred.

Daniel Morten Simonsen at Arhus University in Denmark has written the only dissertation, that we know of, in the area of internal crisis communication. His dissertation *Organizational resilience from a communicative perspective: Sensemaking and organization in crisis* (2015) deals with the concept of resilience that has gained attention in management and crisis research over the last decade (see Chapter 6, page 96). In this context, resilience is an organization's capability to adapt to and handle a crisis situation once it has arisen and to subsequently learn from the crisis itself. Resilience can be viewed as a counterpart to anticipation, which involves trying to predict the future and thus being prepared for the various events that may arise. While both these facets are important, resilience is of particular importance in complex situations and organizations. The dissertation's research question is, "How does communication contribute to the continuous process of creating organizational resilience in a crisis situation?" Through interviews and observations, Simonsen studied soldiers who participated in two so-called hunting exercises, in which the soldiers are exposed to acute physical and psychological pressure. These two exercises are examples of extreme situations and gave Simonsen the chance to study how the soldiers handled and solved the different crises that arose. Simonsen's dissertation demonstrates how fundamental communication is to the soldiers' understanding and construction of the situation; together they create a "rational" universe wherein interpretations are seen as equally meaningful as the events themselves. By defining the situation together in a certain way, the soldiers can create a plan of action. Simonsen's advice to practitioners is to try to expose existing ideas and expectations, as they strongly influence processes of sensemaking and thereby how an organization manages and resolves a crisis situation.

What is common between the previously cited studies is that they not only focus on the acute phase but also on the other crisis phases.

They also go beyond the traditional management orientation and include co-worker perspectives in their research. Furthermore, the importance of continuously working on developing strong relationships between co-workers and other interested parties is emphasized. We nevertheless call for an even stronger emphasis on co-worker perspectives in future research. Far too much crisis communication research is based on studies of communicators and public relations specialists (cf. Taylor, 2010), while the "regular" co-worker is overlooked. Even in several of the previously mentioned studies, it is the crisis communicators or the crisis managers who have spoken of how internal crisis communication works.

Having reviewed earlier research on internal crisis communication, we could conclude that (Heide & Simonsson, forthcoming) there is a need for more research on informal and horizontal communication between co-workers during crises and how co-workers commonly create meaning. Yet another interesting area for future research is co-workers' communication on social media and the relations to and impact on internal communication.

The co-workers – a special and important actor

Maureen Taylor (2010), an American professor in strategic communication, maintains that an organization's capacity to handle a crisis in relation to media, clients, patients and other external parties is a result of internal relationships and communication processes. Through communication with each other we develop an understanding of the present situation, which strongly impacts how we choose to act and to treat our colleagues as well as individuals and groups outside our own organization. Taylor also points out that small organizational problems can easily develop into crises that affect external interests. Also, communication has an important role in discovering and solving these problems.

> Internal communication is a lever that helps to prevent crises, supports appropriate reactions, minimizes damage and eventually produces positive results
>
> – Mazzei et al. (2012, p. 32)

In a time when openness and transparency are the mantras of nearly all organizations, it is obvious to question whether organizations should separate their internal and external communication during a crisis. Should transparency not mean a free flow of information and that internal information is available for external parties? What we would like to argue, however, is that openness and transparency are not necessarily counteracted by disseminating different information internally and externally, by using a different tone of voice in relation to different audiences or by using different channels internally and externally. Quite the opposite, these differences in communication are what often make target groups feel appreciated, involved and as though the communication holds significance and meaning for them personally.

In their groundbreaking article, Finn Frandsen and Winni Johansen (2011) discussed several factors that clearly differentiate co-workers from other stakeholders:

1 *Type of relationship:* Co-workers in an organization have a specific agreement or contract with the organization as an employer. For example, there is both a judicial relationship that regulates what co-workers may communicate, and an economic relationship wherein co-workers receive their salary in compensation for their work. Even other interested parties, such as customers, can have an agreement with the organization, but these are agreements of an entirely different and less extensive nature.

2 *Interests:* Related to the preceding point, co-workers have different interests than those of external parties. When one's employer lands in a crisis, co-workers find themselves in a situation wherein their job, source of income, working conditions and motivation are at stake or are subject to change. Co-workers' interests in relation to the organization affect their need for communication, their interpretations of what is communicated and often even their explanations regarding the emergence of the crisis (see Coombs, 2007).

3 *Identity and degree of identification:* Co-worker identity is quite clearly more strongly linked to the organization in comparison with other, external stakeholders. For example, a strong organizational culture can often lead to the organization becoming a large part of its co-workers' identity. In other words, the co-workers identify themselves with the organization. If a co-worker feels excluded or forgotten, or if they don't receive important information during a crisis, this can affect their loyalty and their desire

to defend the organization or contribute to the management of the crisis. Some organizations have strong subcultures connected to different professions or functions, and this "social identity" (Alvesson, 2013) can be stronger than the organizational identity itself. For example, there is a wide variety of different identities in hospitals, such as doctors, nurses and professors, and any threat to one's own profession can clearly directly and negatively impact the threatened personnel's loyalty to the organization.

4   *Both senders and receivers:* The traditional view is that the co-worker is as a receiver of information, an object that should be informed and reassured. This is despite the fact that that in many organizations, concepts such as dialogue, participation and co-worker engagement are strongly emphasized (Heide & Simonsson, 2011; Zerfass & Franke, 2013). The view of co-workers as passive receivers concerns internal communication in a general sense, but it runs especially true when considering crisis communication. However, the fact is that co-workers talk about their feelings, attitudes and experiences with their colleagues and their family, friends, neighbors and other personal contacts. It's also not unusual for co-workers to talk in the media or else express their opinions on social media. In their role as senders or messengers, co-workers play an important ambassador role; whether this role is positive or negative often has a huge impact on the outcome of a crisis.

Altogether, this shows that co-workers have a stronger and more multifaceted role in relation to the organization relative to other interest groups. Frandsen and Johansen (2011) say that co-workers are "closer" to their organizations than other stakeholders are. We would take this one step further and claim that co-workers actually *are* the organization. With this in mind, we contend that organizations have every reason to focus their communication internally during a crisis and that, in this context, the communication needs to be more comprehensive, interactive and detailed and be characterized by a more direct and personal appeal in comparison with communication aimed at other parties.

The goals of internal crisis communication

The first thing to ask when working strategically with crisis communication is what you actually want to achieve with the communication. In our experience, this question is seldom sufficiently thought through, and it is thus easy to get stuck in certain communications patterns. Sturges (1994) argues that in both theory and practice we have been all too focused on providing quick and accurate information during the acute phase of a crisis. Consequentially, crisis communication has been reduced to a defensive and short-term concept, but it should, instead, be seen from a wider perspective –in terms of time frame, the course of the crisis, content and goals. Sturges (1994) has proposed three different goals of crisis communication, which, from an internal perspective, can be described as follows:

- *Providing instructions:* Say what is expected of the co-workers with the aim of avoiding harming both people and objects as much as possible. What should the co-workers do in order to protect both themselves and others? For example, is there a need to evacuate buildings, where can drinking water be found and where can people take shelter (Coombs, 2019)?
- *Contribute to processing the crisis:* Help co-workers to process and manage the psychological effects of the crisis, including stress, insecurity and anxiety, among others. One way this can be done is by reducing uncertainty. Giving base information on what, when, where, why and how things are happening in connection to a crisis is crucial for handling the psychological effects of a crisis. Another way to handle anxiety is by communicating what an organization does in order to solve a crisis and also what it can do to prevent the repetition of similar crises in the future (Coombs, 2019).
- *Strengthen loyalty and engagement:* By increasing a co-worker's identity with an organization, you make their role as an ambassador relating to a crisis much easier. During "normal" circumstances, engaging co-workers and creating a company identity are the two most important goals of internal communications. In times of crisis this goal is just as important but even more difficult. Johansen et al. (2012) contend that the type of crisis (product failure, rumors, etc.) and the managers' behavior will impact how the co-workers' engagement and pride in the organization will change as a result of the crisis.

We can also identify a fourth important role of internal crisis communication:

- *Creating organizational crisis awareness:* Cultivate both a culture and a leadership that promotes a focus on crises. A crisis-aware culture means, among other things, a culture where mistakes are seen as learning opportunities instead of failures in which the guilty parties are pointed out. It also means a culture that can easily detect weak signals of happenings that may develop into crises. In Chapter 5, we develop the theory of so-called High Reliability Organizations and how such organizations have developed a high degree of crisis awareness.

We discovered in our interviews with hospital personnel that it was more or less taken for granted that crisis communication means making sure that the right people are in the right place so that nobody gets hurt and so that the hospital can continue to provide care to the patients. In other words, hospital crisis management was focused on giving instructions. Although post-crisis processing also occurred, it was most often connected to giving psychological help for handling stress and trauma. Questions regarding loyalty and engagement were on the agenda, but we didn't see that they were connected with crisis management and crisis communication.

 Questions for discussion

Many authorities, municipalities and county councils have published their guidelines for crisis management on their website. Look up and read through an organization's guidelines and consider:

- Is the goal of their internal crisis communication clearly stated?
- Which types of communication and communications goals are emphasized?
- Is there any breadth in the goals (compared with the four roles described earlier)?

Different phases require different types of internal communication

Sturges (1994) notes that different types of communication should be used during the different phases of a crisis (see Chapter 1, pp. 23–27, where different phases of a crisis are discussed). We further argue that

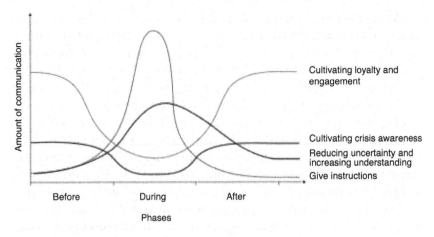

Figure 3.1 Internal crisis communication over time.

different actors have different roles in relation to the different goals of crisis communication (see Figure 3.1).

Before the crisis: During this phase, the two last mentioned goals are the most important: cultivating loyalty, engagement and crisis awareness in the organization. Studies point to the importance of properly functioning internal communication during "normal situation" and the establishment of trusting relationships between management and co-workers. If co-workers have a good relationship with their employers, they tend to act as ambassadors during a crisis (Mazzei et al., 2012). Conversely, it has also been found that if good employer–co-worker relationships don't exist before the crisis breaks out, ambassadorship and pride in the organization are extremely difficult to create, regardless of any communication efforts surrounding the crisis (Mazzei, 2010; Mazzei & Ravazzani, 2011). The organization's communications function is also important in creating a strong organizational identity – not least by creating messages and building a structure of internal media and meeting forums. Although senior management teams and managers also play an important part in creating pride, dedication and loyalty, the professional communication function together with the human resources function should be able to take overall responsibility and support the managers in this undertaking. The nearest manager plays a key role regarding the fourth goal of crisis communication: creating crisis awareness and openness around mistakes and problems. Within the university hospital we saw several examples of how specialists in quality issues could be a great support to managers and help create transparency and a willingness to talk about mistakes and so-called deviations.

During the crisis: During this phase, the focus should be on instructional communication; that is to say, the first objective of communication in the earlier list. Communication with the goal of cultivating commitment should be avoided or, in the very least, reduced during this phase. Spreading information during the middle of a crisis that promotes an organization or shows to its co-workers how amazing the management is can be counterproductive and perceived as cynical and unprofessional. During the acute phase of a crisis, the emphasis of communication must be on minimizing harm to the victims. From an internal perspective, the co-workers who have direct contact with external stakeholders should be prioritized, as they are one of the most important channels outward. Key players in the instructive communication are managers and the top management team, but communicators can play an important supporting role in the provision of information.

After the crisis: As soon as the most acute phase of the crisis is over, organizations need to begin providing information aimed at helping concerned parties to process the events. As mentioned earlier, this can be a matter of telling your co-workers what is being done to solve the crisis or to avoid and be better prepared for these events in the future. Reducing uncertainty and increasing understanding of what has happened are key. Again, both managers and communicators have an important role in this. Post-crisis processing can also be undertaken on an individual level by means of a psychologist. Although the manager nearest to the co-worker can be of help here, in more serious crises, professional psychological help may be needed. Following the crisis, it is once again important to emphasize communication that cultivates co-workers commitment and strengthens organizational identity. Summing up the events and showing the lessons learned from them is another way to create crisis awareness.

In this section, we have advocated for a broader perspective on the crisis communication objective, emphasizing that different goals and types of content need to be emphasized during the different phases of a crisis. It should be noted that there are no clear-cut differences between the different types of communications goals (Johansen & Frandsen, 2007; Mazzei & Ravazzani, 2011). For example, information about what has happened, how to act safely, who should take on which tasks and so on helps both to create clear instructions and to reduce uncertainty and thereby help the affected process the events. It can

also be argued that well-managed instructional communication during the critical phase of a crisis will help co-workers feel pride and
loyalty surrounding their own employer. Nevertheless, we argue for
an increased focus on communication that helps to cultivate organizational identity and pride as well as crisis awareness. We consider
a prerequisite to strategic crisis communications that organizations
work with all these communications goals in mind.

Chapter 4

Leaders and co-workers – perspectives and roles

CRISIS RESEARCHERS OFTEN EMPHASIZE leadership as a decisive factor in successful crisis management. A large part of leadership research, as well as research on crisis management and crisis communication, is based on a perspective with the leader as a person in focus instead of leadership as a relational, mutual process. Recent research on leadership, however, has begun to consider co-workers as co-leaders or co-producers in leadership. In line with this new thinking, we not only discuss leaders' roles but also the roles of co-workers and communications in the crisis context.

This chapter begins with a discussion on leaders and leadership. We discuss issues like, what is the difference between management and leadership associated with crises? What are the crisis leader's primary tasks? What can different perspectives from research on leadership teach us about successful leadership in the context of crises? The latter part of this chapter deals with the importance of co-workers and how the culture of an organization creates different views and values about the role of co-workers.

Divided research

Researchers in the field of crisis communication have, from our perspective, not been interested in leadership and the role of the manager in the crisis context. Although there are exceptions (Seeger et al., 2003; Ulmer, 2012; Ulmer et al., 2011), leadership is not yet a key part of crisis communication research. For example, in *The Handbook of Crisis Communication* (Coombs & Holladay, 2010) there is no chapter dealing with leadership or the role of leadership and communication. Looking at the broader area of *crisis management,* management and leaders have naturally had a bigger place, but that area is characterized by a rather narrow view of communication. Mitroff (2001) emphasizes that crisis communication is only a small part of crisis management, and that crisis communication is primarily something reactive. Such an assertion testifies to a view wherein communication is equated with media management and response strategies (see the information-oriented approach discussed in Chapter 2). Looking into a third field of research, leadership research, we have seen an emphasis on leadership in stable situations rather than leadership in situations of crisis and turbulence (Baran & Scott, 2010; James, Wooten, & Dushek, 2011). In summary, research on the communicative aspects of crisis leadership is therefore lacking.

Some of the communicative advice given to managers and leaders can be seen as quite naïve. Leaders are often told to tell the truth as soon as they notice that a crisis is beginning (Mitrof, 2001; Ulmer et al., 2011). Even if we assume that it is the leaders' view of the truth that needs to be told, it can be hard for them to know what the truth is and to give an opinion on it at an early stage. Often a crisis is accompanied not only by an explosion of information and communication but also by large informational gaps and difficulty in determining what is correct information (Rosenthal et al., 2001).

Management versus leadership in relation to crises

Mitroff (2001) posits that in connection to crises, there is a marked difference between crisis management and crisis leadership:

> The term crisis management is synonymous with reacting to crises after they occur. It implies a low-level management activity. For many, crisis management is identical with putting the "best spin" on a crisis. In contrast, crisis leadership is proactive and high-level. It's about doing everything humanly possible – doing all the "right things" – to prevent crises before they happen.
>
> (p. 19)

Mitroff's distinction between crisis management and crisis leadership holds parallels to the difference between the narrow and broad approach to crises that we describe in the second chapter. Crisis management can also be described as something *episodic*: a crisis blows up, and for a certain period, managers and leaders are forced to exert operational crisis management. Crisis leadership, in contrast, is *continuous*, strategically orientated toward managing the underlying system failures that crises often express ('t Hart et al., 2001).

The distinction between management and leadership has long been an important and debated divider in leadership research in general (Grint, 2005). Management is often described in terms of administration and orientation toward the here and now, that is to say, toward what is already known. The management team is formally constructed and includes work with the bureaucratic and administrative processes connected with planning, budget, systems, technical problems and control. Leadership is instead focused on development, the future and the unknown. It is based on the ability to create shared concepts and ideas, and a strong and cohesive organizational culture (Alvesson & Spicer, 2011). However, Alvesson and Spicer (2011) argue that this distinction is problematic. Leadership is presented as glamorous, challenging and desirable, whereas management seems to be boring and somewhat banal. Critics also believe that this difference is excessive and that managers – regardless of the organizational level – have to devote themselves to both leadership and management (Alvesson & Spicer, 2011; Jackson & Parry, 2011).

We agree that leadership and management are integrated with one another. However, we do still believe that the term crisis leadership highlights the need for a wider, more strategic, long-term approach to crises. Mitroff (2004) points out that we live in a systematic age, a reality that is becoming increasingly complex and wherein everything integrates into one cohesive system. Crises do not occur because a small part of a system fails, but instead, they occur because the entire or a major part of the system does not work (Mitroff, 2001). According to Mitroff (2004) we continue to deal with problems as if we were living in a machine age wherein everything – not least our organizations – can be divided into different parts or units and can be dealt with independently of one another. Mitroff claims that crisis management is no longer enough in our increasingly complex world and that we also need crisis leadership.

We can see examples of "machine thinking" in our study of the hospital. A number of different functions were set up on the crisis management area: a crisis and disaster management group, a psychological disaster relief group, emergency responders linked to emergency room units, coordinators of risk and vulnerability analyses and

Table 4.1 Crisis management and crisis leadership.

Crisis management	Crisis leadership
Emphasis on operational work	Emphasis on strategic work
Reactive – aimed at making the best of the situation when the crisis is underway	Proactive – aimed at preventing the crisis from even happening.
Episodic – occurs during a limited time frame, when the crisis is at its worst	Continuous – is ongoing as an integrated part of day-to-day operations
Views the organization as a machine – possible to separate into defined functions	Views the organization as a system – made up of co-dependent elements

quality coordinators involved in deviation management. As we have understood it, these units work relatively isolated from each other and are not integrated into a central crisis management function. Earlier researchers have argued that large complex organizations need elements of both centralization and decentralization (Perrow, 1977); this is something we are prepared to agree with. Decentralization is needed to create a flexible system wherein knowledge close to the core business is readily available, whereas centralization is necessary for coordination and strategic work. Crises need to be a part of the senior management's agenda – otherwise, it is highly likely that crisis work can become fragmented and reduced to a tactical and reactive task.

The differences between management and leadership related to crises can be summarized as in Table 4.1.

This summary points to why it is unreasonable to rely solely on either management or leadership. Both are needed, but what we often neglect and need to develop is crisis leadership. In the next section we investigate the most important tasks for a crisis leader.

The crisis leader's 10 tasks

As crises are becoming more and more complex, it becomes increasingly important for individuals in leadership positions to have the ability to properly handle crises. Boin, Kuipers, and Overdijk (2013) claim, however, that there are seldom any thorough evaluations or analyses of crisis leaders. In order to facilitate such evaluations, they have compiled a list of the 10 tasks that crisis leaders should undertake:

1   *Early recognition:* Have the leaders created work conditions that facilitate the discovery of deviations, threats and risks?

2   *Sensemaking:* Have the leaders created, facilitated and applied methods and processes for collective sensemaking?

3   *Making critical decisions:* Have the leaders carefully considered which decisions they will make, and have they made these decisions on the basis of an appropriate process?

4   *Vertical and horizontal coordination:* Have the leaders monitored and evaluated different forms of vertical and horizontal coordination? Have they facilitated effective cooperation and intervened when the cooperation fell apart?

5   *Connect and disconnect systems:* Have the leaders actively examined the state of critical systems and the connections between them? Did they seek out expertise on these systems?

6   *Meaning making:* Have the leaders presented a clear interpretation of the crisis and explained how they plan to handle it?

7   *Communication:* Have the leaders actively cooperated with their communication professionals to ensure that quick and correct information is passed on to those affected?

8   *Rendering accountability:* Have the leaders tried to give a transparent and constructive description of their own behavior before and during the crisis?

9   *Learning:* Have the leaders invited reflection about the consequences of their chosen management methods, and have they encouraged negative feedback?

10 *Enhancing resilience:* Have the leaders actively engaged in crisis preparations?

Boin and his colleagues point to a series of tasks that can be expected of management within an organization to prepare themselves to face a crisis. The preceding list can be used not only to evaluate leadership in crises that have already occurred but also to discuss the tasks in order to clarify roles and expectations before a crisis.

> **?** **Questions for discussion**
>
> Are these reasonable tasks? Are they congruent with your expectations of how a leader should behave during a crisis?
>
> Are there other tasks that should also be included on the list?
>
> Keep in mind that a list of this kind can act as a solid base for organizational members to reflect on what was good and bad with a crisis that has already occurred.

Some researchers argue that it's one thing to be a good leader in everyday work, and a whole other thing to be a good leader during a crisis (Muffet-Willett & Kruse, 2009). Although it may definitely be true that not all leaders can handle crises, several of the tasks in the preceding list are not unique to crisis situations (see van Laere, 2013). Most of these tasks can be applied to other situations and events – not least profound organizational changes and development work. However, compared to other situations, crises are characterized by a greater degree of uncertainty, increased time pressure and a greater threat of serious negative consequences for the organization. We would therefore argue that it is the terms and conditions of the work situation – rather than the tasks themselves – that distinguish crises leadership from day-to-day leadership.

In the next section we discuss the different perspectives within leadership research in order to deepen our understanding of the crisis leader's communicative role.

Different perspectives on leadership

Research on leadership has been undertaken from a number of different perspectives that all hold differing assumptions on what leadership is, and which issues are most pertinent to focus on. A rough distinction can be made between four different perspectives:

- One that focuses on leaders' *traits and characteristics*
- One that focuses on the leaders' *style*
- One that focuses on the importance of the *situation* (contingency theory)
- One that focuses on the *communicative* aspects of leadership

Perhaps the most important role of the crisis leader is to handle the uncertainty and confusion that arises during a crisis. Each perspective emphasizes different aspects of leadership in crisis situations, and we briefly discuss how the different perspectives relate to the leader's role in managing the uncertainty associated with crises.

Characteristics, style and situation

Until the beginning of the 1940s, research on leadership was dominated by an endeavor to define the primary characteristics of effective leaders. The idea was that leaders are born, rather than educated or developed. Characteristics such as physical traits (e.g., height), general abilities (e.g., intelligence) and personality (e.g., humor and integrity) were studied (Jackson & Parry, 2011; Seeger et al., 2003). However, the search for a specific set of characteristics that characterize the effective leader proved fruitless. The results of these studies were contradictory, and it was difficult to find one universal set of characteristics between effective leaders (Parry & Bryman, 2006). Seeger et al. (2003) believe, however, that crises constitute a more specific type of situation and that it is possible to distinguish certain characteristics that are particularly important for a crisis leader. The ability to handle stress and maintain calm in chaotic, exposed situations is especially important to them. Other characteristics important to a crisis leader are the ability to think critically and to see things from a variety of perspectives.

The other perspective emphasizes the leader's style, that is to say, what they *do* rather than who they *are*. Here, two different styles can be distinguished. The first is the relationship-oriented style, which means that the manager focuses on developing a good friendship with his or her co-workers, being available, and holding a high level of trust among his or her followers. The second style is task-oriented, which means that the manager carefully defines what the co-workers are expected to do and how to do it (Parry & Bryman, 2006). Other styles that can be distinguished are the democratic and authoritarian styles. The democratic leader is in a position to take information from different sources, and involves many in the decision-making process, whereas the authoritarian leader is characterized by quick decisions and the exercising of direct control (Seeger et al., 2003).

Crises may appear to be situations where authoritative, task-oriented leadership is required. Seeger et al. (2003) argue that authoritarian leadership may be appropriate in certain crisis situations, as these situations often require action and quick, clear decisions. At the same time, they stress how important it is that crisis leaders take care not to isolate themselves and to collect information from co-workers and other sources. Gilpin and Murphy (2008) are even more skeptical about authoritative leadership. They claim that complex organizations require leaders capable of creating a climate where co-workers can organize and solve critical situations on their own. We are inclined to agree with Gilpin and Murphy and argue that regarding crises, researchers have tended to overestimate the importance of authoritarian leadership and underestimated the importance of crisis leaders listening and distributing power to others. Although acute, urgent crisis phases may require quick decision-making in order to deal with uncertainty and create action, these situations are often limited in both time and space, and coping with the situation in general is something for more than just the senior executives and managers to take on.

The third perspective – the contingency perspective – emphasizes the impact of the situation on effective leadership. Once again, researchers have been interested in a relationship versus task-oriented leadership style, but according to this perspective, the styles work differently in different situations (i.e., the idea is to match different styles of leadership with different types of situations). In line with what we have already said about complex, knowledge-intensive organizations, we want to issue a warning about placing excessive emphasis on the authoritarian, task-oriented leadership style in the face of a crisis. Crises are multifaceted situations and often require focusing on both structuring tasks and nurturing relationships. A leader who does not show his or her emotional support, interest and concern in relation to co-workers, as well as external stakeholders, is in a position to significantly obstruct crisis management (Seeger et al., 2003).

? Questions for discussion

Think of an organization that you have worked in or know well. What kind of leadership – authoritarian or democratic – would work best for that organization during a crisis?

Which leadership style is "normally" sought after in that organization?

What are the potential disadvantages of using an authoritative leadership style during a crisis, if a more democratic leadership style is normally used?

Leaders as visionaries and managers of meaning – the heroic leader

The three perspectives described earlier all share a strong emphasis on the leader as a person and co-workers as passive objectives of influence (Collinson, 2006). Society is greatly fascinated with leaders, and we often tend to have an expectation that leaders have an almost super-human ability to solve problems and produce positive results (Sims, 2010; Ulmer et al., 2011) – not least in times of turmoil and crisis. Leaders in successful businesses are often given a hero status, while leaders in organizations that fail are turned into scapegoats who need to be replaced by a "rescuer" who can save the organization.

During the 1980s, a new perspective of leadership emerged, emphasizing visions, change and the organization's ideational world. Parry and Bryman (2006) use the term the *new leadership perspective*, while Sveningsson and Alvesson (2016) call it the half-new perspective, to mark the fact that the perspective is no longer so new. This perspective entails a number of theories, called transformative, charismatic, symbolic and visionary leadership (Levay, 2009; Parry & Bryman, 2006; Sveningsson & Alvesson, 2016). The common denominator of these different labels and approaches is formulated by Jackson and Parry (2011, p. 31) as follows:

> Together these labels revealed a conception of the leader as someone who defines organizational reality through the articulation of a vision, and the generation of strategies to realize that vision.

The new in this perspective consists primarily of the view of the leader as a manager of meaning (Smircich & Morgan, 1982). Leadership is not primarily about controlling behaviors and exercising direct control but, rather, about influencing co-workers' ideas of what is happening inside and outside their organization. The emphasis on sensemaking is closely linked to the emergence of knowledge-intensive organizations, where what controls and holds the organization together consists of visions, values and goals rather than orders, directives and rules (Heide & Simonsson, 2011). This new/half-new perspective on leadership has an increased interest in the communicative aspects of leadership; in order to make sense of and influence other peoples' ideas and approaches, the leader must communicate.

From a crisis perspective, the question of sensemaking is highly relevant. Unexpected and dramatic events imply a deviation from stability, which triggers an active search for meaning (Maitlis & Sonenshein, 2010). That which is new and deviant in a turbulent situation initiates a sensemaking process in which we try to answer questions such as "What's actually happening?" "What will the consequences be?" and "What should I do?" At the same time, crises and other ambiguous situations hold a series of strong and negative feelings such as fear, uncertainty and panic, which complicates the opportunities to make sense and understanding (Heide et al., 2012).

Collaborative leadership – the post-heroic leader

Just as the early perspectives in leadership research, the new perspective emphasizes the leader as a person. The spotlight is still placed on the leader/the sender, but instead of the person's characteristics or style, emphasis is now placed on the leader's charisma and ability to formulate convincing and engaging messages. Fairhurst (2001) claims that leadership is seen as a monologic process; the leader makes sense for the co-workers rather than together with them.

In recent years, more and more researchers have begun to question the idea of the powerful heroic leader, and critics have started emphasizing leadership as a mutual, relational process. This alternative approach often goes under the name "post-heroic" (e.g., Alvesson & Spicer, 2010; Sveningsson & Alvesson, 2016). The post-heroic perspective highlights the more common aspects of leadership such as listening, conversing and encouraging, rather than magnificent visions and powerful speeches. Sensemaking is still at the core, but in line with the idea of leadership as a mutual process, it is assumed that both managers and co-workers contribute to making meaning and influencing how reality is perceived. Co-workers are thus seen as active subjects/communicators and co-leaders. The monologic view of communication is replaced with a dialogical approach that emphasizes how meaning is negotiated in a social process rather than transferred from leader to co-worker (Fairhurst, 2001; Simonsson, 2011).

Muffet-Willett and Kruse (2009) argue that collaborative leadership – where co-workers participate in developing the organization's direction and values – pave the way for an ability to act independently and successfully in times of crisis. Ancona, Malone, Orlikowski, and Senge (2007) state that it is time to dispel the myth of the complete leader, and to instead embrace the incomplete leader – a leader who does not always have total control over everything but who understands when it is time to listen to others or let others do their job. The incomplete leader knows that leadership is present throughout the organization and is likely to involve others' perspectives in a process of continuous sensemaking.

A crucial characteristic of the post-heroic perspective is that co-workers hold a much more central place in the leadership. However, there are different variations of this perspective, which can be placed along a continuum (Jackson & Parry, 2011). On one end, there is a more "radical" viewpoint, wherein the distinction between leaders and co-workers is questioned and alternatives to the traditional managerial leadership are pushed forward (e.g., collegial, upward, or network-based leadership). Based on this view, everyone has the potential to become a leader, and almost all actions can be seen as leadership (Alvesson & Spicer, 2011; Shamir, 2007). This more radical attitude can be criticized for underestimating the power and "resources" that come with a more formal position of power. At the more conservative end of the continuum lies – in our opinion – a more balanced view, in which the formal leader's importance is noticed at the same time as leadership is seen as a mutual (though not always symmetrical) process that involves several different actors (Simonsson, 2011). Formal leadership positions hold an interpretative prerogative and an expectation to influence the ideas and viewpoints of others. However, co-workers' views on what is happening inside their own organization are far from merely a result of the words and actions of their managers. Co-workers can interpret and reinterpret leaders' messages, influence each other's perceptions of ideas and the ideas and understandings of their own managers.

In the following section we discuss leaders' ability to make sense through framing, and in the next and final section we look at the role of co-workers in the process of sensemaking.

Sensemaking through framing

Unexpected and exceptional events, such as natural disasters, product recalls, workplace accidents, heavy cuts and so on, threaten an organization's day-to-day stability and therefore trigger a sensemaking process. In situations of uncertainty and ambiguity, we leave our routine sensemaking, and actively look for new meanings and understandings (Balogun & Johnson, 2004; Weick, Sutcliffe, & Obstfeld, 2005). In the acute phase of a crisis, there is often a need for clear, easily accessible information to answer a number of concrete questions, such as who has the mandate to make decisions, how many are injured, or how to evacuate a building. This type of information consists of a number of "facts" that are quite unambiguous, but many of the questions that arise during a crisis have no given answer and cannot be answered in terms of any specific facts. As often mentioned in this book, crises are complex phenomena where much has to be interpreted and explained in order to answer questions such as "What's happening?" "Why is that happening?" "What should I do?" and "What are the consequences?" Crises are thus characterized by an inherent ambiguity, and we can expect co-workers to actively search for meaning in connection with crises (Baran & Scott, 2010). What senior managers and one's nearest manager say and do in such a situation often has a significant impact on how co-workers interpret and perceive the situation.

Framing is a term that is often used to denote the symbolic actions a leader undertakes to influence others' perception of reality (Deetz, Tracey, & Simpson, 2000; Fairhurst, 2001; Fairhurst & Sarr, 1996). Naturally, words are not capable of changing a physical occurrence (i.e., stopping a natural disaster), but by using a specific tone and telling an event in a certain way, the leader can influence how the event is interpreted and, ultimately, how people respond and act in a crisis situation (Seeger et al., 2003).

What, then, does framing mean more concretely? First, it is about the language and symbols (stories, illustrations, metaphors, etc.) we use when communicating. Through language leaders can help co-workers to categorize different events and thus create some sort of meaning and order. A situation described by a leader as "catastrophic," "radical," or "disastrous" will presumably be interpreted as being much more serious than a situation described by using the words *disturbance, incident* and *turbulence*. Ethically, a leader should, of course, choose the words that best reflect the current situation, but it is rare that one clear word choice exists, so it is important that leaders consider how they want the situation to be perceived when choosing their words.

Second, framing may mean that an event or experience is related to a particular context. A word, an act or an event usually becomes meaningful only in relation to something else. The introduction of new requirements for reporting errors and deviations can be perceived completely differently depending on whether it is presented as part of the general implementation of new public management, or if it is related to an attempt to create an open culture where people can learn from their mistakes. New public management (NPM) is the umbrella term for a set of ideas exported from the private sector to the public sector with the hope of overcoming a conventional and ineffective administration (Berlin & Kastberg, 2011; Simonet, 2008). More specifically, NPM has resulted in an increased emphasis on management by objectives, evaluations, resource utilization, competition, accounting and transparency. In other words, framing is not about communicating "objective" information but, rather, about refining and transforming information into a meaningful message (Smircich, 1983).

However, many researchers point out that managers often miss the opportunity to influence and facilitate sensemaking processes through framing (see Fairhurst & Sarr, 1996; Deetz et al., 2000). In their studies on change, Alvesson and Sveningsson (2015) have found that the manager's communications tend to be characterized by a kind of symbolic anorexia. Managers' communication tends to be characterized by abstract, neutral words, with no connection to the co-workers' own situations and experiences, resulting in a lack of meaning or commitment. In our own study of the hospital, we found not only some examples of the absence of framing but also clear examples of attempts at framing, which we discuss in the two following sections.

Absence of framing – an example

The hospital that we studied, generally speaking, placed the strongest emphasis on their external communications (especially the press, the media and its external website), which resulted in senior management and line managers missing the chance to influence and facilitate their co-workers' sensemaking process. The lack of focus on internal communication was evident in the organization's crisis management plans, in which press officers were assigned a clear role while communicators responsible for internal communication were not highlighted (Heide & Simonsson, 2014a). The interviews also indicated a relatively narrow view of who internally was affected by an organizational crisis. The units directly impacted by a crisis were those who were considered to be most important to reach with information. Other co-workers in the organization appeared to be, at least at times, given more or less the same information as external stakeholders. We argue that if co-workers get the same information with the same address and tone as external stakeholders, there is an obvious risk that co-workers' loyalty and willingness to act as ambassadors will decrease.

What also proved to be problematic was that the hospital's internal communication channels could not compete with external media coverage in terms of speed or scope of publication. Co-workers said that they often used regional media websites in order to find out what was happening within their own organization in the events of accidents or other crises. It is quite obvious that hospitals and other public organizations are under heavy media coverage, and the hospital we studied was no exception; one interviewee even claimed that "there are fewer days that we are not in the newspaper than days that we are in the newspaper."

Our point is not that executives and communicators can avoid negative media reporting in times of a crisis. However, we do see a great need to comment internally on external media coverage. If this is not done, the external media can enjoy "free" influence over how the co-workers understand the situation. A lack of internal communication in a situation characterized by worry and insecurity can, bluntly put, mean that leadership grants its internal communicative role to the external media.

We also found other examples of missed opportunities by the managers to influence the perceptions of their co-workers. In the second chapter of this book, we discussed the co-workers' experience that the hospital as an organization is in a crisis situation. One of the interviewees, however, said that the managers did not want to talk about "crisis":

> There is currently a crisis in the hospital with tight fiscal measures and we close certain units. For example, we are now caring for many patients who belong to another clinic [. . .] But one avoids the word crisis. As a boss you don't want to worry.
>
> (Nurse)

On one hand, it is logical that, as a manager, you do not want to create a sense of crisis and concern. That said, if senior management and other managers do not acknowledge the experiences of their co-workers and talk about it, the co-workers are left on their own in their communication about it. The managers therefore leave the sensemaking process to the co-workers, thus losing the chance to exercise their leadership. In the next section we present a theory that can explain this sort of lack of communication.

Construction of problems – example of an active attempt at framing

Keith Grint (2005) has developed an interesting theory on how decision-makers and managers actively construct the perception of a situation in order to legitimize a certain form of action. Grint's theory is based on different types of problems situations and can contribute to an increased understanding of leaders' communication. Grint (2005) distinguishes among three different types of problem situations related to different types of leadership:

- *Wicked problems* – very complex problems characterized by a high degree of uncertainty. One solution often generates new problems and there are no clear right or wrong, only worse or better solutions. Wicked problems require *leadership* (rather than management; see the earlier discussion in this chapter) with the ability to handle the unknown, that which has not yet been experienced. The leader's role is to ask the right questions rather than delivering the correct answers. There are no given answers to the questions, and it is therefore important the leader encourages the cooperation required to arrive at the best possible solution (see also Baran & Scott, 2010; Fairhurst & Sarr, 1996).

- *Tame problems* – complicated problems but have often occurred before and are not characterized by as much uncertainty as the wicked problems. There is an end point where the problem can be considered solved, and the decision-makers' role here is to exercise *management* by laying out a clear process for solving the problem.

- *Critical problems* – constituted by an accident, a natural disaster or similar (in other words, a traditional crisis) and requires quick and clear decision-making. Critical problems are, of course, not easy to solve and can have devastating consequences, but at the same time they are characterized by the least degree of uncertainty compared to the other two problem types. The task of the decision-maker is to act as a *commander* by quickly moving to action and providing answers as to what should be done. The commander may not always know the correct answer, but this is not communicated to his or her followers, and there is no time for planning processes or asking questions. The acute aspect of critical problems thus legitimizes authoritarian leadership with the ability to exert direct coercion, if required.

Grint (2005) claims that decision-makers tend to legitimize their actions on the basis of a convincing description of the current problem. The way in which the problem is described tends to be in line with the decision-makers' preferences for different types of power and leadership roles. This is what Grint calls *the irony of leadership*: most decision-makers avoid defining a situation as wicked, as the ensuing leadership role is significantly more difficult than the role of manager (tame problems) and commander (critical problems). Grint's definition of leadership implies that leaders have no answers to give, that the solution to a problem requires strenuous efforts and a long time to implement and that co-workers must be a part of this effort (which is not always popular for a leader to communicate). It is therefore easier to create legitimacy and acceptance for the roles of manager and commander – although it may not really be the most effective for the organization.

In the previous section we gave examples from the hospital study in which we found that senior management and managers were not meeting the co-workers' experience of working in an organization in crisis. We interpret this as an expression of Grint's irony of leadership. The organization is in a very complex problem situation (a wicked problem) without any obvious or simple solutions. The solution not only is in the hands of management but also requires action at a political level, both regionally and nationally. If senior management members had chosen to communicate the situation in such a way, they would have to have dealt with the difficult form of leadership, which, according to Grint, decision-makers are often unwilling to undertake.

We have, on the other hand, found examples of problematic situations at the hospital that management has chosen to describe as tame, with an inclination toward critical. In line with Grint's theory, we also saw that management then took the role of manager and commander. We conducted observations of some meetings regarding how to maintain adequate care capacity and quality during summer vacations. During these meetings, senior management used words such as *emergency* and *critical* to describe the situation, and it was clear that they wanted to mobilize a common responsibility among managers and co-workers to solve the problem. Senior management appointed working groups, plans and strategies were put in place to address the lack of staff, special routines and meetings were initiated to manage problems and staff were informed that they may be required to work overtime and move their holidays. Expressed in Grint's terms, we can clearly see examples of management here, wherein processes were created to solve problems, but at the same time senior management indicated that they face or at least stand to face a critical problem in which the staff may be commanded to cancel or move their holidays. We are not saying that the situation was not critical or catastrophic, but what is interesting here is how the framing and description of a particular situation legitimizes a more authoritative leadership.

The importance of the co-workers

Managers and leaders definitely have a central communications role during a crisis. At the same time, as previously mentioned, there is growing criticism of the focus on leaders as single individuals with hero-like properties. Having too much faith in managers as powerful individuals implies a view of co-workers as passive recipients rather than as active and independent communicators. Raelin (2015) points out that having too much faith in the importance of a manager is likely to hamper the energy and creativity of organizations and society at large. As the number of competent, knowledgeable co-workers who have more expertise in specific subject areas than their managers increases, it is, in turn, becoming increasingly important to see these co-workers as active subjects. In the coming sections we give some examples of the importance of the co-workers in sensemaking processes.

Co-workers in High Reliability Organizations

In the next chapter we discuss the theory of High Reliability Organizations (HROs) – organizations with complex and risky operations, where mistakes can have devastating consequences. The theory clearly highlights the co-workers' central role in dealing with unexpected and unpredictable situations. The primary difference between HROs and other organizations is the ability to capture weak signals of something that may develop into a crisis. Although it may seem counterintuitive, a strong response to these weak signals is often necessary, in order to handle the unexpected (Weick & Sutcliffe, 2007; it is more typical to give weak responses to weak signals and strong responses to strong signals). Weak signals are usually noticed first in the daily routines related to the core business, for example, in the number of patients placed in the "wrong" department, in meetings with customers where problems with product quality become apparent, when technical problems increase in production and so on. It is often the frontline co-workers who are closest to these weak signals and who are first able to detect them. Managers need to therefore be interested in and listen to the co-workers' experiences in order to properly respond to the weak signals with a strong response. Weick and Sutcliffe (2007) describe this as *sensitivity to operations*, which is one of several principles that are especially pertinent to HROs. In the hospital study, the staff said they reported fewer mistakes and deviations due to a lack of feedback on deviation reports and an increasingly pressured employment situation. At the same time, the number of complaints filed by patients increased, which can be interpreted as weak signals growing stronger, but the co-workers felt that they were ignored or did not get an adequate response from managers. One of the interviewed managers said that he and his colleagues realized the importance of feedback on deviation reports, and he said they would work more systematically with this in the future. At the same time, the same manager felt that it was tough to discuss complaints from patients with a stressed and severely overworked staff group. This reminds us that each manager must have support from his or her own direct manager and that the organization, as a whole, must be sensitive to what is happening with the "front staff."

Another principle that characterizes HROs is *deference to expertise* (Weick & Sutcliffe, 2007), which means that those who have the most expertise on the matter make the decisions. Weick and Sutcliffe stress that decision-making migrates in the organization, in search of the person with the greatest expertise in the field in question. Thus, authority in the HRO is linked to knowledge and expertise rather than to a formal position in a hierarchy.

In our study of the university hospital, we found some contradictions regarding deference to expertise. Hospitals, in general, can be seen as clear professional organizations with a number of professional groups: doctors, nurses and administrators (including economists, communications, human resources specialists, etc.). The doctors tend to dominate, and this can be interpreted as the principle of respect to deference as it seems to apply to that particular group but not to other professions of the organization. The interviews show that there is a loosening of doctors' dominance, which can be seen through an effort to work more in teams, and with nurses moving up and taking managerial positions more and more often (see Berlin & Kastberg, 2011). At the same time, we find examples in our study that the doctors and the medical logic continue to dominate. One such example was found when we observed a number of management meetings during the summer period. The purpose of these meetings was to evaluate and manage current patient care capacity on a daily basis. At each meeting, a so-called healthcare coordinator (holding a position as a nurse) checked and reported on the number of available hospital beds – that is to say, those in this position were most knowledgeable about current care capacities. At one point, the healthcare coordinator broke into the conversation at the meeting by saying, "Forgive me, but even if we use all the available beds in orthopedics, we won't have enough space . . ." The initial apology indicates that the coordinator did not feel like a part of the group and the decision-making power, which may not be so strange in a group of divisional managers, chief physicians and others. At the same time, our interpretation in this case is that the healthcare coordinator in question had the most expertise and thus had an important role to play in decision-making.

Organizational culture and co-workers

How co-workers react and communicate in relation to a crisis is closely related to the organization's culture. Organizational culture is encapsulated by mental, ideational phenomena, that is to say, how we perceive and value our reality (Alvesson, 2013). We have previously featured examples of how a so-called medical logic dominates the hospital we studied. This logic – which means that the norms and values of doctors and nurses tend to dominate over different management models – can be seen as a central component of the organizational culture and has, among other things, colored how a crisis is defined in the organization. In the previous section, we highlighted how hospitals are composed of strong professional organizations, which are of major importance for co-worker identity and organizational culture (see Alvesson, 2013, for a discussion about the relationship between organizational culture and identity). Co-workers who belong to strong professions, such as doctors and researchers, identify themselves more with their own profession than with the organization for which they work. Loyalty is tied first to their profession and then to their organization. A clear example of this was given in an interview with a doctor during a holiday period when the management had regular meetings to discuss personnel and care capacity. The doctor said that they did not receive any information from these meetings:

Doctor:	I never know what is said at the 1 o'clock meeting. The only thing we notice is that we are one man short, as our head doctor disappears to go to the meeting.
Interviewer:	Do you need information? Would you want to know what was said, or how things were going?
Doctor:	Whether or not we have available beds shouldn't affect me in my treatment of patients. So I'm not really interested in that information, because I know that it may affect me, and I may start to take bigger risks with my patient's health if I feel that I'm under pressure, as in such situations there can be a pressure to send patients home instead of keeping them in the hospital.

The preceding conversation can be interpreted as an example of how one's professional responsibilities are being prioritized over the organization, as many different interests need to be balanced at once. Identity and loyalty are given to the role as doctor, not to the hospital as an employer. The doctor thus does not look for information about what is happening within the organization at large or within his own department.

Some organizations can be characterized by a strong organizational culture wherein co-workers identify with the organization. Co-workers see themselves, first, as a part of, for example, Apple or Ikea, and, second, as an economist or engineer. In these organizations, co-workers are often more willing to be active ambassadors for the organization as a whole. Methods such as "lines to take" – concrete suggestions on how co-workers can answer hostile or adversarial questions – can be a successful tool in these organizations. However, at a university or in other organizations with a strong professional culture, these methods may trigger a reaction in the co-workers of "you cannot come here and tell me what to say or not to say."

Being a manager or leader in a strong professional organization seems to be a challenge, to say the least. A basic prerequisite for exerting influence is trust between the managers and co-workers. The doctor's reaction discussed earlier may be based not only on a strong identity and integrity as a doctor but also on a lack of confidence and trust in the decisions and approaches that management tries to convey. During the interview, the same doctor mentioned that he felt that management was often too positive in how they conveyed information. He felt that more balanced internal communication, in which both positive and negative information was shared, would have created a more trusting relationship. Relationships characterized by trust and confidence are often portrayed as a sort of "crisis vaccine" in crisis communication research. Trusting relationships cannot in and of themselves prevent crises, but strong trust between management and co-workers means that co-workers are more prepared to engage both before, during and after the crisis (see James & Wooten, 2005).

 Questions for discussion

Have you as a customer, consumer or patient ever experienced that co-workers have acted as either a positive or a negative ambassador regarding a crisis situation?

What can managers and communication professionals do to promote positive ambassadorship among their co-workers?

Chapter 5

Anticipation – the art of looking for weak signals

IN THIS CHAPTER we discuss the importance of organizations continually searching for signals or signs of changes that could lead to a crisis. The focus of the chapter is to discuss error management as part of an organization's crisis management. We begin by presenting previous research in the field and subsequently illustrate with practical examples.

Everyone makes mistakes

"Human beings, in all lines of work, make errors" (Kohn, Corrigan, & Donaldson, 2000, p. ix). An important starting point in the crisis-aware organization is accepting that we all make mistakes every now and then and sometimes even often and regularly. Accepting that mistakes are a natural part of everyday life is the first step toward changing and improving; if we turn a blind eye to mistakes, or sweep them under the carpet, we will never be able to develop. This holds true for both organizations and individuals. The Swedish psychologist Anna Kåver (2004) demonstrates this by insightfully emphasizing the importance of acceptance for people who have landed in a crisis situation. Kåver believes that people in crisis will only be able to act once they have accepted the situation, as only then can different forms of mental blocks disappear, and people can open themselves up for solutions Kåver (2004, p. 39) writes: "being able to see everything clearly and handle the situation by moving to action, even though you may feel like avoiding the situation or giving up, that is what I call 'acceptance through action'." Mistakes happen constantly and can be perceived as only being negative. However, if viewed positively, mistakes can be considered important lessons and as opportunities to prevent a major crisis from occurring.

Many organizations, however, have a culture that has "zero toler-ance" for mistakes, which, in turn, leads to organizational members developing strategies to cover up and hide their mistakes. Perrow (1994) poses the rhetorical question of why safety work is not a higher priority in organizations. He answers the question himself and claims that very few decision-makers are punished for not put-ting safety first, even after an accident. On the other hand, they are punished if they do not prioritize profits, market shares and orga-nizational reputation. This means that mistakes are not discussed at all in the organization. In such an organization, leaders seem to have too much faith in the "rational man" who, through access to information and knowledge, can make optimal decisions. However, as we have learned from Herbert Simon (1957), who in 1978 received the Nobel Prize in Economics, people have a limited capacity to be rational. It is quite simply impossible to collect all the thinkable information and furthermore impossible to cognitively function all that information. Rather, we can, in practice, make decisions based on a limited amount of information and try to make this information meaningful so we can better understand the situation (Weick, 1995).

According to professor in business administration Nils Brunsson (1982), much research has focused on finding models for how organi-zations can become more rational, but most decisions in organization have a lot of elements of irrationality. Brunsson even claims that there needs to be some irrationality in an organization in order for them to operate. This is called *action rationality*. Our ability to make quick and effective decisions is impaired if we are constantly looking for the optimal, rational decision. Weick (1995) emphasizes that it is only retrospectively that we can understand and make sense of a situation. Many situations and conditions are so complex that it is impossible to understand or think through the best possible decisions in a ratio-nal way. For example, doctors cannot directly diagnose a patient with complex, difficult symptoms of disease, but instead, they first test some medications based on the symptoms that the patient displays. Once the patient has been treated with this medicine for a certain amount of time, the doctor will try to understand and diagnose the disease again. What happens then is retrospective meaning creation to understand the situation. If the patient is not responding to treatment and medicine, the doctor will try any other medicine that could help. Correspondingly, when work is done within an organization, mistakes are important "data" from which important future decisions can be made.

Mistakes at the hospital and error management

Mistakes are a given part of complex, modern organizations. One example of an organization where mistakes happen continually is the hospital. Most of us have a perception of healthcare as an institution where rational, wise decisions are made and very few mistakes occur. This is, unfortunately, a misconception, as mistakes in healthcare are very common. An American study shows that medical mistakes cause as many as 100,000 deaths per year (Kohn et al., 2000). This study, published by the Institute of Medicine, concludes that medical mistakes are the eighth-leading cause of death in the United States. The report became a bit of a watershed, as it clearly showed that medical mistakes were not connected to technology or technological error but, instead, to a lack of consideration for patient safety (Kim & Newby-Bennett, 2012). The situation in a small country like Sweden is no better, with approximately 3,000 patients dying annually from avoidable mistakes (Thornblad, 2012). This corresponds to one domestic plane crashing every week for a year, which clearly indicates the magnitude of these mistakes.

Naturally, the situation in the Swedish health sector has been heavily discussed. It is almost exclusively discussed in a negative light, with focus on factors such as constant budget cuts, overcrowded emergency room wards, burned-out staff and all the subsequent mistakes that occur. Everyone in Sweden has read about closing clinics and long waiting times and the high risk of illnesses getting worse, or even leading to death, that patients undergo while waiting in queue to see a doctor. As a response to this debate, the Swedish newspaper *Expressen* has started a Twitter feed #akutkollen (#emergencywatch in English) where patients can report their negative experiences with Swedish healthcare. The Swedish tabloid *Expressen*'s initiative is supported by, among others, the Swedish Healthcare Association, which is an idea-based political organization aimed at influencing political decisions that can lead to good care. Since 2008, the Association of Hospitals has awarded the "Fisherman of the Year" award to "a person who stood up for democracy and freedom of speech in healthcare for the benefit of patients and doctors."[1]

The American report from 2000 on deaths due to medical mistakes contributed strongly to the fact that work on improving patient safety has become a mantra in healthcare. This is applicable to the Swedish healthcare system, where officials are working intensively to improve patient safety, which can also be seen as an answer to all the criticisms that the healthcare system has undergone. One of the ways to work on improving patient safety is deviation management: the purpose of this is to record mistakes, encourage mistake learning and reduce future mistakes, thus improving patient safety. Deviation management is closely linked to crisis management in an organization, as mistakes can lead to a crisis developing, and deviation management has a particularly close connection to internal crisis management.

What does the research say?

In recent years, researchers (such as Christianson, Farkas, Sutcliffe, & Weick, 2009; Goodman et al., 2011; Hunter, Tate, Dzieweczynski, & Bedell-Avers, 2011; Sutcliffe, 2011) have increasingly started to recognize mistakes as a resource for crisis management, learning and development. Among other things, researchers have been interested in the feedback that co-workers give, as seen by, for example, Bisel and Arterburn (2012), as one of the best resources in a warning system, as this information can be used for organizational development. The big challenge in organizations is how to properly handle all the information generated by co-workers.

The premise in most research is that the combination of many small mistakes together can have serious consequences and eventually lead to an organizational crisis; this means that every small mistake made by an individual is a risk to the organization (Maitlis & Sonenshein, 2010). One of the first researchers who focused on mistakes in organizations was the American professor of sociology Charles Perrow at Yale University. According to Perrow (1984), up to 70 percent of all

---

1 Friska sjukvårdspriset och Årets Visslare [eng. *The healthy healthcare award and Fisherman of the Year*] www.slf.se/Foreningarnas-startsidor/Yrkesforening/Sjukhuslakarforeningen/Om-oss/Friska-sjukvardspriset-och-Visslaren/

accidents and incidents in an organization are due to human error. For this reason, it is quite common to blame other individuals when mistakes happen. However, pointing out one person as a scapegoat for a mistake is a grave error, as most mistakes in an organization are caused by a complex chain of events and therefore represent systemic failures (Reason, 1990).

There are several different definitions of organizational errors. One definition comes from Goodman et al. (2011, p. 153): "the actions of multiple organizational participants that deviate from organizationally specified rules and procedures and that can potentially result in adverse outcomes for the organization." Another example comes from Hofman and Frese (2011, p. 3), who claim that organizational members' actions are "wrong when they inadvertently fail to reach their goal, if this mistake could have been avoided." In other words, organizational member's actions can only be considered a mistake when there is a goal related to the consequences of that action. *Risk*, which is a related term, should not be seen as a synonym to mistakes. The difference is that mistakes are things that can be avoided, whereas risk is an intrinsic, natural and unavoidable part of a situation and can therefore be analyzed before any actions are underway (Hofman & Frese, 2011).

In the traditional crisis management literature, organizational mistakes are seen in an entirely negative light, despite the fact that organizations, without mistakes, would not exist (Clarke, 1999). In addition, we learn and develop as people through our mistakes, whereas when we do something correct, we get confirmation that we have done the right thing but do not develop in any way. The well-known social psychologist Leon Festinger (1983) emphasizes that all development is a product of human error. The opportunities for learning are much greater in organizations where mistakes are not viewed as negative or threatening. According to Huber (2004), organizational learning can be seen as a process where organizational members revise their performances, which, in turn, leads to improved performance and increased results for the organization. The new knowledge creates new repertoires that improve the organization's ability to handle similar situations in the future (Christianson et al., 2009). This also reduces the risk of future crises.

There is also a long tradition of research on healthcare organizations (e.g., Berlin & Kastberg, 2011). In this literature, the majority of the research has been aimed at micro-related events, such as trying to reduce the number of mistakes. Macro-events, such as organizational culture and leadership, have, on the other hand, not received this same level of focus (Ruchlin et al., 2004).

The normal accident theory (NAT)

There are two central theories regarding mistakes in organizations, which focus on macro factors such as leadership and organizational culture: the normal accident theory (NAT) and the high reliability organization (HRO) theory. These theories are often presented as being completely different and with different objects of focus (Sagan, 1993). One of the pillars of NAT is that serious accidents will always occur in complex, risky systems, despite all possible efforts to avoid them. This goes against HRO theory, which believes that learning from mistakes by focusing on security, and through a decentralized structure wherein organizational members are *empowered* to make important decisions. Below we will describe the theories in more detail.

Charles Perrow (1984) penned the term NAT. Perrow is interested in systemic complexity and the connections between the different components of a system. According to Perrow, it is impossible to avoid system accidents in a complex, closely connected system, such as process industry or hydropower. In fact, the risk that accidents will occur is actually higher in such a system, as nothing is perfect, and in such a complex system, even a small mistake can be deeply integrated and can lead to a major accident (Perrow, 1994). Complex, tightly interwoven systems can be contrasted with linear systems such as production lines, which are predictable, possible to stop, and, in most cases, visible. Such predictability does not exist in a complex system. If a mistake or accident occurs in a linear system, it usually does not occur again. According to Perrow, the solution is to make organizations more loosely coupled, that is to say, the departments in the organization become more independent and not as interdependent. This gives a bit of wiggle room, as individual units are not so closely linked. In turn, this reduces vulnerability, and organizational members become more flexible and are able to make faster decisions. Loosely coupled systems are, simply put, better equipped to adapt to changes. Examples of loosely coupled systems include universities and public administrations. The various units are, to a certain extent, governed by rules, regulations, instructions and so on, but they also have a high degree of independence. For example, negative events within one department at a university do not affect the other departments, and there is a fairly high degree of freedom for the institutions in relation to one another.

 Questions for discussion

Perrow, who authored NAT, argues that organizations that are based on loosely coupled units are less vulnerable and more flexible, which makes it easier to manage mistakes and avoid big crises.

Are there any disadvantages to loosely coupled organizations? What are these disadvantages, and how can they be reduced?

The HRO theory

In the following sections, we go deeper into HRO theory, as we believe that most organizations can learn something in crisis management from HROs. This theory also focuses on "softer" aspects such as culture, learning and sensemaking.

Although it is widely understood that mistakes can happen, and machines and other equipment can break down, certain organizations *cannot* afford to make very serious mistakes (La Porte & Consolini, 1991). In these organizations, mistakes can have disastrous consequences. Examples of HROs include nuclear power plants, chemical processing industry, air traffic management systems and military missile facilities. Most laymen in modern society trust that these systems work flawlessly. Weick and Sutcliffe (2007) emphasize that what HROs deliver first, before a certain product or service, is *trust*. This can make or break not only these organizations, but also normal organizations, as without trust, organizations have little chance of survival in the long run.

What is remarkable is that HROs exist, despite the fact that the majority of research demonstrates that mistakes will occur sooner or later in complex systems (Perrow, 1984; Sagan, 1993). A group of inter disciplinary researchers at Berkeley found this phenomenon especially interesting and have closely studied such organizations since the late 1980s. This group includes Todd La Porte (professor of political science), Karlene Roberts (professor of organizational behavior and industrial relations), Gene Rochlin (professor of the Energy and

Resources Group) and Karl Weick (professor of organizational behavior and psychology). The first publications on HRO came in the early 1990s (e.g., La Porte & Consolini, 1991; Roberts, 1990).

Safety culture

An important starting point for HRO theory is that an organization has a culture that is characterized by dependability and where co-workers feel safe. If an organization has such a culture, it is possible to discuss and reflect on the risks, mistakes and near-mistakes that have happened. The main argument with HRO theory is that successful organizations have great potential and possibilities to learn from their earlier mistakes, and this is a result of a *safety culture* (La Porte, 1996; Weick, 1987). Such a culture is characterized by common norms, shared perceptions, working methods and informal traditions surrounding crisis and security thinking. Furthermore, such an organizational culture is characterized by a high degree of flexibility and interest in learning and development (Ruchlin et al., 2004; Sutcliffe, 2011). The term *safety culture* was coined in the late 1980s by the International Atomic Energy Agency in Vienna, which was tasked with investigating the Chernobyl accident, which occurred on April 16, 1986. Then, the term was used to try to explain why the accident occurred, as the explanation was beyond simply human or technical error (Guldenmund, 2000). There appeared to be a lack of a safety culture, where technicians ignored warnings and shut down safety systems.

The traditional, rational decision-making models, not least in management literature, are based on the premise that the environment is stable and more or less unchanging. Reality rarely works this way, and organization members need to make sense of what is actually happening before a decision can be made (Weick, 1987). In order to form an opinion, a culture with certain norms and values is also required, which helps organizational members to make decisions. Sensemaking cannot happen without a culture with certain decided norms and values, which helps organization members to make decisions. Weick (1995) emphasizes the need for both centralization and decentralization in order for a complex system to work. However, it is difficult to design such a system, and instead, centralization can be replaced by standardized action routines or *organizational culture*. If the organizational culture works well, it offers rules for how members will act and thus has a governing and coordinating effect.

In all organizations, organization members' stories hold a special weight, as they help to maintain organizational culture:

> Stories remind people of key values on which they are centralized. When people share the same stories, those stories provide general guidelines within which they can customize diagnoses and solutions to local problems.
>
> (Weick, 1987, p. 125)

Stories are a natural way for people to communicate (Bruner, 1990). Stories have also proved to be important for our understanding, sensemaking and learning in an organization. By recounting stories to each other, we learn how we and other people understand the world. Some researchers, such as Galpin and Sims (1999), argue that until we have created a story that gives a certain structure and meaning to an event, there is nothing to remember. Stories in organizations have a socializing function, as they teach new organizational members the informal rules, norms and values that guide the organization (Orr, 1996). This contributes to the survival and spread of knowledge in the organization. The stories that exist in an organization can be seen as a form of organizational memory to which co-workers are an important resource (Sims, 1999). Weick (1987) points out that stories are also an effective tool as they register, compile and describe situations that are difficult and complex to linearly reproduce.

An organization as large as the university hospital is clearly full of stories. These stories differ depending on if the staff work on the medical/nursing side of things or on the administrative side. As previously mentioned, the medical field dominates the university hospital, which, in turn, means that stories related to medicine are the strongest. In the following quotation, we have an example of a story that we often encountered in our interviews:

> And that's how it is. The patients we have will always come first. It's not like I can say "Sure, but you know what? Can you wait for me while I sit down and write this deviation report," while the patient is looking over my shoulder asking: "What should I do now? What am I waiting for? When should I go in to the ER?" Patients have a thousand questions that need to be answered, that's what I'll do first.

This story exemplifies that the medical personnel put their patients first and that they are most loyal to their profession and its prevailing values. While this is neither strange nor wrong, it can be a bit problematic from an organizational and leadership perspective. The stories that dominate an organization ultimately drive what is valued and prioritized and therefore what ultimately happens within the organization.

Learning from mistakes

What characterizes high reliability organizations is that goal fulfillment and efficiency are emphasized as much as security and reliability (La Porte, 1996). In many high reliability organizations, deviation management works. The organizations that are successful in their reporting of deviations do it by

- avoiding the all-too-common "naming, shaming, and blaming";
- having open discussions about mistakes;
- statistically analyzing data about mistakes;
- education and training programs; and
- overseeing a system for reports (Stock, McFadden, & Gowen, 2006).

However, the most prominent feature of high reliability organizations is the acceptance and expectation that mistakes are made on a regular basis and that co-workers are trained to identify, learn, adapt and reorganize on the bases of mistakes made. Instead of isolating the mistakes of individual events, co-workers try to learn and generalize the knowledge for the organization as a whole (Reason, 2000). It is, however, no small feat to realize and accept that mistakes and failures happen and that perfection is an unattainable goal (Ruchlin et al., 2004). All organizations develop different mental models for how to handle things, which contribute to organizational inertia and a reluctance to process new information and rethink how things are done.

All people act and react based on their own perceptions and meaning-creation (Weick, 1995). The meaning that co-workers create is formed on the basis of their own interpretative frameworks. Interpretive frameworks are built based on previous experiences, interests, education, norms, values and, not least, the dominating organizational culture. Organization members' incentive to detect mistakes is effectively reduced in organizations where co-workers are punished or scapegoated for making mistakes, or where mistakes are swept under the table and kept quiet (van Dyck, Frese, Baer, & Sonnentag, 2005). From this sort of behavior, a norm can develop wherein mistakes are ignored or repressed, and the same mistakes occur over and over with no organizational learning or development. There is also an obvious risk that the mistakes will contribute to serious accidents, which could ultimately become an organizational crisis.

An important part of improvement in organizations is continually reflecting over and discussing what happens in an organization. Then, co-workers have a better chance at uncovering weak signals of changes that, in the worst case, could turn into a crisis (Weick & Sutcliffe, 2006).

Anticipation and resilience

In the book *Searching for safety*, the American political scientist and risk researcher Aaron Wildavsky (1988) expresses two universal strategies for improving safety in an organization: *anticipation* and *resilience*. Both anticipation and resilience are characteristic of HROs (Weick & Sutcliffe, 2007). Anticipation is the ability to predict and prevent various hazards from developing. According to Weick and Sutcliffe, anticipation is formal preparation for the unexpected. Resilience refers to attempts to deal with hazards once they have developed and manifested. One of the oldest definitions of resilience comes from the anthropologist Mary Douglas and political scientist Aaron Wildavsky (1983, p. 196): "Resilience is the capacity to use change to better cope with the unknown; it is learning to bounce back." Resilience is thus the organization's capability to learn and recover from a crisis, as well as the ability to use previous knowledge to prevent a new crisis from occurring. We will now leave the concept of resilience and return to it in Chapter 5, "Resilience." In the following section we continue the discussion on anticipation.

Anticipation in an organization is, in practice, when organization members are aware of mistakes, generalizations and events. It involves, among other things, trying to predict negative events from weak signals of changes. When mistakes occur in the organization, it is important to note these, discuss them, and in the best case change this negative development. Furthermore, anticipation involves stopping the development of events that can lead to an accident or, ultimately, a crisis. Weick and Sutcliffe emphasize that organizations that have a culture that advocates anticipation have much better chances of avoiding crises. An important starting point for HROs is that the earlier a deviation can be detected, the greater the chances of handling it. The challenge here is that, as Weick and Sutcliffe (2007) write, the earlier one tries to detect a mistake, the harder it is to find it.

An organizational culture that is characterized by crisis awareness also requires modern leadership that promotes coworkership and understands the value of an open communication environment, where co-workers' voices, knowledge and experiences are taken seriously (see Ulmer, 2012).

Our experience shows that cooperation and relationships between entities and different levels is one of the biggest obstacles and challenges to safety and crisis work. In most organizations, negative and counterproductive "silo thinking" is pervasive. These silos tend to live their own lives and develop their own norms, values and goals. Like many other hospitals, we found that there are many *mental silos* among administrative and medical staff at the university hospital. Hospitals are usually referred to as professional organizations with a high proportion of specialist staff, who work independently of one another in relation to their clients (Mintzberg, 2009). Another name for professional organizations like this is knowledge companies (Sveiby, 1990) or knowledge organizations (Alvesson, 2004). A distinguishing factor of these organizations is that the specialists have a relatively high amount of power and are considered difficult to handle. These specialists view professionalism as being connected to their own skills and competencies and not to the management rules, values, norms and routines (Svensson, 2002). Therefore, administrative and medical personnel have different rationalities and ideals, which complicates how crises and crisis management are viewed. The medical staff has higher status, and certain preferential rights are noted in the crisis plans. Focus is placed on certain medical crises and not on other possible crises linked to trust and leadership. Apart from this silo, the traditional silos between different clinics and divisions are also present.

Two strategies for improving safety in an organization

Anticipation – an organization's capacity to predict and prevent various hazards from becoming a reality *beforehand* by noticing mistakes, failures and weak signals of an upcoming crisis.

Resilience – an organization's possibilities and capacity to learn and recover from a crisis, as well as use knowledge from previous crises to prevent new ones from occurring.

Organizational silence and upward negative information

Co-workers need to be able to feel secure when reporting mistakes or deviations from the normal in an organization (Weick & Sutcliffe, 2007). Co-workers are a huge resource with wide expertise. They are constantly observing and are sensitive to changes within an organization. If organizations do not want their co-workers to ignore or attempt to ignore mistakes and deviations, then they need to actively encourage deviation reporting, reward reports and, above all else, not penalize mistakes.

Organizational silence is a phenomenon that has been increasingly noted in recent years. Such self-censorship is cultivated in organizations whose culture is closed, negative and non-democratic. Organization members keep quiet even if they want to share their experiences, knowledge, points of view and so on, as they want to protect themselves from different forms of punishment. These punishments can include being shut out, disapproval, poorer career prospects, lower salary and so on. Organizational silence can therefore be, in part, explained by a closed and nonpermissive communications climate (Hayes, Glynn, & Shanahan, 2005).

All societies, organizations and social groups have some sort of dominant opinions. These are so strong that other, alternative modes of thinking cannot come forward. People with opinions that go against the grain tend to keep their thoughts to themselves; this is often because they are afraid of isolation and exclusion from the group.

Literature on organizational silence typically refers to *the spiral of silence*, first penned by German political scientist Elisabeth Neumann-Noelle (1993) in her book *The Spiral of Silence*. This theory explains why certain opinions dominate a society, organization, or group and why opinions that go against the grain are pushed down. According to the spiral of silence, people are extremely sensitive and responsive to which opinions dominate a social setting. These dominant opinions oftentimes prevent people from daring to express their own views for fear of being excluded from the group. As most of us are social creatures who want to belong to a group and be well-liked, we often tend to go with the tide: we simply adapt our own opinion to that of those around us.

? **Questions for discussion**

- Have you been a part of a group or organization where the spiral of silence was prevalent?
- What were the consequences of this silence?
- What would have been necessary to end the spiral of silence and create a more open climate?

When organizational silence was first studied, researchers saw silence as a sign of loyalty to an organization. Silence was, in other words, the same as having everything in order (Shojaie, Matin, & Barani, 2011). This is in line with research on *consensus*, that is to say, agreement within a group of people, which is the goal of communication. For example, this is a goal that the German communications researcher Jürgen Habermas (1995) advocates. Other communications researchers, such as the American professor in organizational communication Stanley Deetz (1992), argue instead that consensus should only be found as a temporary milestone when coherence is not developing. He believes that it is when we disagree in our arguments and opinions with each other that we develop and new understandings and knowledge can be formed. In other words, Deetz sees *dissensus* as an important goal of communication. Managers have an important role in creating a communications climate wherein different views are discussed in an open and mutually respectful manner. It is only when these conditions exist that it is possible to fully work with anticipation.

The literature also states that it is crucial in a successful organization that different and opposing information reaches leadership (Cheney, Christensen, Zorn, & Ganesh, 2011). In the HRO, members of the organization are encouraged to make their voices heard, give their opinions and point out mistakes and failures. This differs greatly from the average organization, where zero tolerance of mistakes and failures is usually dominant. When we make mistakes, we often keep them to ourselves without telling those around us, especially not our bosses. This behavior is reinforced if managers do not understand the educational value of lifting and discussing mistakes. Research unfortunately shows that many leaders have a clear tendency to perceive co-workers who deliver divergent or negative information as less competent (Burris, 2012), and consequentially, these co-workers do not receive the same support and encouragement as other co-workers. When all is said and done, the negative and closed communication climate is consolidated in an organization until new leadership that views mistakes differently and understands the importance of a permissive and supportive communication climate is in place.

In order for co-workers to be able to tell their bosses about mistakes, and for continuous reflection and learning to be possible, a certain communications culture needs to be in place where *upward negative information* from the co-workers to the senior management is encouraged and rewarded. This area has typically been neglected in research, though interest in this research field is now growing. Although researchers such as Roberts and O'Reilly (1974) and James Grunig (1975) had, as early as the mid-1970s, highlighted the need to study this form of communication, it was only in the mid-2000s that interest among researchers came about. The researcher who has presumably written the most on upward negative information is the English researcher in organizational communication Denis Tourish (e.g., Tourish, 2005; Tourish & Hargie, 2004; Tourish & Robson, 2003, 2006). His arguments include the importance of supporting upward negative information so that managers and management teams get a more varied, nuanced and true picture of reality. This, in turn, leads to better conditions for making better decisions. A side effect of promoting opportunities for co-workers to criticize is that managers tend to be more appreciated by their co-workers.

> People who refuse to speak up out of fear undermine the system, which knows less than it needs to know to work effectively.
> – Weick and Sutcliffe (2007, p. 13)

Organizational structure and culture have the tendency to obstruct the upward flow of negative information. Despite this, Swedish organizations have, generally speaking, come further than international organizations, which may be due to the Swedish principle of public access to official records, a small power distance between managers and co-workers and a leadership tradition that is rooted in consent and the right of co-determination. Research has shown that the Nordic model for workplace relationships is an explanatory factor in the equal relationships between managers and co-workers in Swedish and Norwegian organizations (see Skivenes & Trygstad Sissel, 2010). According to these researchers, the open communications climate and shared decision-making power in organizations has a positive effect on the spread of negative information within an organization.

Here we can speak about *symmetrical information systems* (Sutcliffe, 2001). In this case, symmetry stands for equality between co-workers, managers and leadership. It would be quite naïve to believe that complete symmetry could exist in an organization. All organizations, just like society, have different forms of power and excision of power. Modern power theory stresses that we are all subject to power, and we all have power in one way or another, such as when we have special expertise or knowledge that others in the organization need. However, management and leadership always have higher power authority, and there is always a dependency relationship between co-workers and managers. In any case the symmetrical information system is, like James Grunig's (2006) symmetrical communications model, an ideal model and something to work towards. In such a system, the opportunities for dialogue between co-workers, managers and top leadership are high. According to Sutcliffe (2001), this leads to the co-workers having a better understanding of the organization's goals, plans and relationships to important external actors. In the long run, co-workers will have better opportunities to discover important signals of change in their surroundings and therefore strengthen the quality of their sense-making processes. There are enormous amounts of information in an organization's surroundings, all of which can give organization members feedback on what the organization's current situation is. This information can answer questions such as how business currently is going and if a crisis is approaching. What is important here is not simply gathering information but, instead, interpretation; in both society and organizations today, which are characterized by an overflow of information, the big challenge is choosing which information is important. Only after this is done can the information be interpreted, which can, in and of itself, be a challenge. Furthermore, information can be interpreted differently depending on someone's background, position in the organization, interests and so on. Another challenge is that over time, organizations tend to develop different mental models and ideas, which, in turn, create a sluggishness and unwillingness to change when new and contradictory information is presented.

All in all, an organization's capabilities for effective internal crisis management are better when the organization processes and treats the co-workers' knowledge and information as valuable input. This requires, however, that managers listen; in other words, listening is an important trait for managers to work on (see de Bussy & Wolf, 2008; Sigrell, 2011). The importance of being able to listen to other people has long been known in rhetoric. By listening, managers can take in a number of alternative perspectives and, through this, gain opportunities for learning. There is also an ethical side to this – most people consider it to be courteous and respectful to listen and take in the experiences of others.

Managers also have a central role in ensuring the implementation and rewarding of communication about how a crisis is perceived. According to Weick and Sutcliffe (2007), HROs have high capabilities for discovering small deviations that could develop into a crisis early. The organization can conduct proactive crisis management through open and ongoing communication. In these organizations, less emphasis is placed on decision-making than in traditional organizations and more is placed on questioning and interpreting in order to be able to act in an informed manner (Weick et al., 1999).

Advice – how to promote upward negative information
(see Tourish & Robson, 2006)

Be just as critical towards positive information as you are to negative information.

Create forums for informal contact between leadership and co-workers (e.g., monthly breakfast meetings with the CEO and several co-workers).

Frequently discuss the following questions at different managerial meetings:

- Which problems have we been made aware of since we last met?
- What critique have we received for our decisions?
- How much positive versus negative feedback have we received in the past week?
- Are these criticisms justified, in part or in whole?
- How should we react to this criticism?

The great importance of leadership

Something that was very clear in our research on error management and anticipation in the university hospital was the great importance of leadership (Simonsson & Heide, 2018). Co-workers are required to report any deviations, errors, mistakes or "near-accidents" that have occurred, for example, by logging into the deviation reporting system and recording data in a database. These data can include what happened, when it happened, who was involved, the patient's name and what actions were taken, among others. The report is then sent to a reviewer. This task can be assigned to different occupational groups: in some clinics there is a quality coordinator, and in some departments the managers are in charge of this review task. If the reviewer considers the deviation to be serious, an investigation is conducted. The deviation in these cases is also reported to the unit managers, who may take the case up to the next level. The quality coordinator can also decide whether the deviation should be passed onto the individual responsible for all deviations in the hospital.

Research clearly shows that strong leadership is connected to increased organizational learning and willingness among personnel to make their voice heard (Edmondson, 2003). Leadership accepting that mistakes happen, and wrong decisions are made does not necessarily mean that the instance of these mistakes increases. Rather, this attitude from leadership creates that a safe and nonthreatening climate wherein co-workers share their mistakes with leadership instead of trying to hide them. Our study confirms the important role that leaders have in opposing organizational silence and creating a culture that focuses on mistakes from a learning perspective. A nurse that we interview pointed out the following:

> Our hospital does not, generally speaking, have a good reporting culture. It varies a lot between different departments. If leadership encourages you to write deviation reports and also asks for suggestions for improvement [. . .] and if you have a complete loop with regular feedback – then you have a good culture.

In our interviews, we found a challenge that the hospital faces, in that there are no sanctions against those who do not report deviations. Thus, many perceive the deviation report as something voluntary and optional. The chief physician at the hospital compares this to how deviation reports work in the aviation industry:

> In all aerospace and related industries, there are proper conse-quences for those who do not report, for example, if a technical error has been identified. But with us, there are no consequences for the individual if you do not follow the rules and report devia-tions and mistakes. This is a part of our problems.

Another problem is that the managers' responsibility and role in man-aging the deviation reports is not particularly clear or formalized. Given that the university hospital is a very large and complex orga-nization that is fairly loosely organized, the importance of the man-agement becomes particularly great. There are certainly rules that stipulate that all deviations should be reported, but the absence of sanctions means that a certain organizational culture that promotes reporting is required. As always, managers have an important sym-bolic role as role models and to create the required open and safe com-munications climate. It is important that managers repeatedly stress the *importance of reporting*. However, it is equally important that time is *set aside* at meetings to discuss deviations and collectively come up with solutions.

Feedback from managers to co-workers is also central. Both the managers and co-workers whom we interviewed stressed the worth of feedback on reports that are submitted. One manager stated,

> Our challenge as employer representatives is giving feedback to the co-workers when they have written deviation reports. I think that a large proportion of the co-workers feel that they write report after report, but nothing happens, so the reports are therefore useless. Feedback is therefore key, as otherwise everyone gets tired of send-ing reports in. We have tried to improve our feedback but need to do even better.

Some of the co-workers we interviewed said that it could take up to two months until they get feedback on their reports. This is problematic in two ways. First, this reduces motivation for co-workers to report in the future. Second, this reduces any possibilities to investigate the reports. Some interviewees also expressed that the feedback they received was often standardized.

Most organizations are faced with the ongoing problem that co-workers feel they are too pressed for time to be able to stop, reflect and learn. Pressure to produce and deliver is high, which, in turn, reduces the windows of time that make reflection and learning possible. At the university hospital, many co-workers felt that they were expected to do increasingly more in increasingly less time, which negatively impacted their ability to report deviations. However, this increased pressure not only meant that the co-workers had less time to write deviation reports but also meant that the co-workers risked making more mistakes in their daily work. Here we see a catch 22. The impression we got from our interviews with emergency room co-workers was that they should write a deviation report every day, but due to time constraints the report could not be prioritized. The nurses we interviewed told us that it had been a few months since that they had last filled in a report, and for some it had been over a year. The nurses also stressed that it can be difficult to know what actually a deviation is when crisis has become a norm for the organization.

Communication and cooperation between different departments, units and sister companies is a challenge for most organizations. Most often, cooperative problem solving and learning work on the local level, but do not spread throughout the organization. This was a particular challenge at the university hospital, where the deviation management system was organized differently within different clinics and divisions. Several clinics had managers on different levels that are responsible for completely different processes related to deviation reporting. In other units, there was a specially designated quality chief or the like who had a specialized and coordinating role within several clinics. This was the case in the emergency room unit on which our study focused. The quality coordinator there was described as a real enthusiast who had been very important in getting deviation reporting on the agenda. She has also been crucial in developing a positive reporting culture and has succeeded in increasing the number of reports. The meta-message that the quality coordinators have endeavored to convey to the co-workers and that seems to have had a positive impact is "don't blame the person, blame the system." The determined work of the quality coordinator to raise the issue of deviation management has led many executives to consider deviations as a standing point in workplace meetings.

Our research also points to the fact that the quality coordinator is better placed to conduct investigations and evaluations. As she worked exclusively with deviation reports, she developed huge stores of knowledge that could be used in her assessments. Furthermore, she was responsible for the quality of several clinics, which allowed her to see common patterns across these units. Many times, the deviations may be related to each other and linked to other clinics, which the quality coordinator could detect based on her position.

In addition, she could act as a liaison and share her experiences and knowledge from one clinic with others. Co-workers stressed that the quality coordinator was not seen as a "threat" in the same way as the closest payroll manager. The co-workers did not feel that it was threatening to report an event when they knew that it was the quality coordinator who read and assessed the report.

Finally, a very common problem for organizations is that organizational learning often only happens on a local level. Our interviews in the emergency room show that learning happens informally when the personnel manage different situations and problems that arise. We also found that managers in the emergency clinic both inform about and discuss recurring and serious problems at their meetings; however, organizational learning within the unit often remains at these formal meetings. In other words, horizontal organizational learning is lacking, and our study shows that it is, in practice, difficult to create aggregated learning within a division or at the overall hospital level (Heide & Simonsson, 2013). We see huge potential in organizations to develop their vertical (from the bottom up and vice versa) and horizontal (between departments at the same level) learning. To focus on learning is, effectively, to work more strategically with internal crisis management, and it is important that someone takes responsibility for, leads, and drives these questions. Within a hospital, this responsible person could be a quality coordinator or someone in a similar role.

Chapter 6

Resilience – the art of managing crises and learning

IN THIS CHAPTER we focus on two crucial processes for surviving an organizational crisis, developing and being successful in the long run – resilience and learning. Resilience is an organization's capacity to manage changes that arise, such as during a crisis or other bigger change. Learning, in this case, is an organization's capacity to create new knowledge out of a crisis, which makes the organization better at handling similar situations in the future and even makes them better armored than organizations that have not been through a crisis.

Resilience

The term *resilience*, which stands for the capacity to recover or resist varying disturbances. Resilience is used to describe recovery in society, organizations and individuals, for example after a difficult illness or trauma. The origin of the word *resilience* comes from the Latin *resilire*, which means to "bounce back," in other words to come back to normal, to how it was before a bigger and decisive change. The word is also used to describe the capacity to adapt to a certain situation and to develop to a new state.

Resilience was first used in the natural sciences in the mid-19th century, as a way to measure the hardness and durability of materials. In the 1950s psychologists began to use the term, but it was only in the 1970s and 1980s that it was used in greater detail to describe people's ability to recover from stress and stress situations. Researchers were then interested in individuals who were particularly adept in their capability to handle difficult situations. Resilience was thus seen as a special trait that people had; some people were considered more resilient than others and were therefore considered to be better at coping with and managing crisis situations (Simonsen, 2015). More recently, resilience has been used in other subjects, such as sociology and cultural geography. Here, resilience has been used, in particular, to describe a society's resilience, that is, how societies handle a crisis and recover afterward. In sustainable development, resilience describes an ecosystem's capacity to deal with earthquakes, forest fires and pollution (Alexander, 2013). An ecosystem with high resilience therefore has a high capacity to recover after a crisis.

Organizational resilience

In this book we are focused on organizational resilience – an organization's possibilities to handle the long-term effects of a crisis and to develop through learning. In other words, an organization's resilience depends on how they handle mistakes and failure *after* they have happened and manage them so that the situation does not exacerbate.

> Resilience is a combination of keeping small errors small and of improvising workarounds that allow the system to keep functioning.
>
> – Weick and Sutcliffe (2007, p. 14)

The term *resilience* was first used in relation to *crisis management* by the American political scientist Aaron Wildavsky (1988) in his book *Searching for Safety*. Wildavsky saw resilience as a complementary strategy for protecting a system (such as an organization), and he placed it against "anticipation" and other forms of "guesstimating," or guessing about what is going to happen in the future. This is not to say that Wildavsky rejected anticipation as a strategy, but he argued that it only worked in certain contexts. According to Wildavsky, anticipation is a perspective that presumes that one central unit in an organization can and should control everything and that large focus should be placed on predicting and preventing potential hazards and risks before they develop into a larger crisis. However, the problem with this perspective is that there are countless potential hazards to predict, and by choosing to focus on a limited number of hazards we take the risk of missing others. Again, here we have a catch 22.

Wildavsky defines resilience as "the capacity to cope with unantici-pated dangers after they have become manifest, learning to bounce back" (Wildavsky, 1988, p. 77). Here, resilience is seen as an adaptive organizational process for handling complex and abnormal situations (Sutcliffe & Vogus, 2003). To a great extent, resilience begins when an organization begins to understand and recognize how past actions were not enough and that new behavior is required. Consequently, resilience begins with sensemaking.

Ambiguity, sensemaking and wise organizations

In a research article in the *Journal of Contingencies and Crisis Man-agement* Weick (2015) emphasizes that it is wise for organizations to embrace and accept all the ambiguity that characterizes complex orga-nizations (see Chapter 3's discussion on individuals who land in a crisis and need to accept the situation to act). Ambiguity is a situation where no given meaning exists. The situation is unclear, polysemantic and several conflict-ridden interpretations stand against one another. For example, an economic recession is ambiguous, as there is no one clear explanation for the recession and no clear solution to the problem. Another example is a trust crisis in an organization due to leadership using company funds for personal uses, such as to go on vacations. The challenge in this situation is sensemaking, to create an understanding for all of what is happening (Barton, Sutcliffe, Vogus, & DeWitt, 2015).

The sensemaking process in all unstable, crisis-like situations – *cosmologic episodes* – starts because the organization members want to create order and meaning in an unclear situation. This applies to all of us when we end up in a situation that we do not understand. Most people consider ambiguous situations to be uncomfortable, and they strive to always understand what is happening and therefore make sense of a situation (Weick et al., 2005). We experience a total loss of control in ambiguous situations, which is something that most of us try to avoid. Carroll (2015) argues that a situation can be ambiguous both due to there being *many different meanings* or because *there is no meaning at all*. Both these situations are extremely difficult, and immense effort is needed in order to make sense.

Ambiguity can be compared with *uncertainty*, which describes situa-tions where information on whether something is right is missing. An unclear situation is not as complex as an ambiguous situation, and any uncertainty will disappear with more, correct information. It is then possible to make better plans and predictions. However, in an ambiguous situation, we are not able to even identify, classify or understand an event, and therefore, we do not know which information we should look for.

According to Carroll, *avoidance* is a typical reaction to ambiguity, and people look for *ready answers* that can alleviate ambiguity and *quick solutions* such as education, placing the responsibility on one specific person or by writing more detailed instructions. Furthermore, Carroll argues that leadership turns to experts and consults those that they hope will have the recipe for improvement in ambiguous and complex situations. Carroll stresses that individuals cannot solve ambiguity alone but that instead organization members can collectively construct shared meanings and explanations; this calms us down and makes it possible to act. Carroll points out that the most important thing is not to search for fault, but to have *ongoing conversations* and discussions and *wide engagement among organization members* with the goal of accepting ambiguity and trying to find different solutions, as well as learning from the contributions that the members make.

> *Ambiguity* exists in situations where there is no given meaning. Ambiguity cannot be solved by simply giving more information, but instead sensemaking is needed, that is to say, building a certain explanation that makes the situation meaningful.
>
> *Uncertainty* exists in situations where the information on whether something is right, or how the situation should be handled, is missing. In order to solve this situation, more information is needed.

In high reliability organizations, organization members discern inconsistencies, complications, details and incompetence, and therefore increase ambiguity. According to Weick (2015), ambiguity increases when people better grasp the situation. Although this may sound paradoxical, Weick argues that the goal is not to solve the complex puzzle, but to accept that it exists and to create an acceptable level of ambiguity. This means resisting the temptation to try to reduce or solve ambiguity through simplifications such as stereotypes ("it's that kind of situation!"), categories or habits. In other words, the problem with ambiguous situations is that organization members use previous, recognizable categories, frames and stories to rationalize events and therefore try to restore order. Weick (1993) stresses that if organization members dare to let go of their frames and tools, then it is possible to change how they think, see alternative solutions and improvise in a situation.

In a master's thesis in strategic communications, Lucas Mathisen Dietrichson (2013) describes how the medical personnel at the university hospital constantly rely on improvisation to solve complex situations. One nurse who was interviewed commented,

> You can have as many plans of action as possible, but they're not what you think about when you're in a tight situation. It's not like you have a plan written down in your back pocket that you can take out and look at.

Dietrichson argues that when one considers how these plans of action are produced and spread within the organization, it is not strange that most plans of action within the university hospital are not considered to be a meaningful support to staff in their daily work. Guidelines are based on a template created by the safety coordinators, which the department heads in the emergency room then go through and approve. The next step in implementation is publishing them on the intranet and encouraging co-workers to look through them.

Improvisation is quite simply something we have to do to solve complex problems. It is not possible to list out and plan all the possible scenarios in advance, and we need to learn that ambiguity is not followed by clarity but, instead, by more ambiguity. Weick (1993) stresses that searching for clarity after ambiguity is hard-earned, as it means discarding a lot of potential information along the way. When we think we have found clarity, order and understanding, we are, in reality, simply not open to alternative solutions anymore. From this, Weick concludes that *reliable and wise organizing happens when ambiguity is seen as a constant, and interpretations are seen as temporary.* Organizations are out on thin ice and at a high risk of undergoing a crisis when the opposite is true – that ambiguity is seen as temporary and interpretations as permanent.

> To be wise is not to know particular facts but to know without excessive confidence or excessive cautiousness. Wisdom is thus not a belief, a value, a set of facts, a corpus of knowledge or information in some specialized area, or a set of special abilities or skills. Wisdom is an attitude taken by persons toward the beliefs, values, knowledge, information, abilities and skills that are held, a tendency to doubt that these are necessarily true or valid and to doubt that they are an exhaustive set of those things that could be known.
>
> – Meacham (1983, p. 187)

In other words, wisdom is an attitude. This attitude requires that individuals be skeptical and reflective and regularly question the information, knowledge and viewpoints that are presented to them as correct. Weick claims that in a constantly changing world, wise individuals are those who do not completely understand what is happening right now, as they have never been in exactly this situation before.

Expectations, plans and blind spots

Resilient organizations are distinguished by a culture of attentiveness. Safety lies at the center of these organizations (Boin et al., 2005). High reliability organizations (see Chapter 5, pp. 85–86) are resilient because they know and expect that crises will happen. These organizations therefore place a strong emphasis on training and exercises, and they ensure that their well-educated co-workers continuously deepen and develop their knowledge. Resilient organizations are also distinguished by their acceptance of the fact that *problem-free organizations do not exist.* As mentioned in Chapter 5, everyone makes mistakes, wrong decisions and misses important tasks that they need to do. We learn from our mistakes, as do organization members. Being resilient means learning quickly and being responsive to negative feedback (Weick & Sutcliffe, 2007)

Weick and Sutcliffe (2007) raise the importance of understanding the expectations that dominate in an organization. These expectations are prevalent in, for example, culture, routines, plans, roles and strategies. Expectations help us to order the world around us and to reach a higher level of predictability. Having expectations grants us a certain structure in our lives and gives us a sense of control. Weick and Sut-cliffe write that routines work in this way: they drive our attention in certain directions, which makes us notice, reflect on and remember specific things. Plans work the same way (see Chapter 1, pp. 21–23), by making organization members look for information that confirms that the plan is correct. However, plans to have a tendency to make people one-track-minded and make it difficult to discover the unexpected – that which is not a part of the plan. Plans are often made on the pre-sumption that it is possible to organize and predict the world around us; it can be difficult to be open for changes and unexpected events if this attitude dominates an organization.

> Plans, in short, can do just the opposite of what is intended, creating mindlessness instead of mindful anticipation of the unexpected.
>
> – Weick and Sutcliffe (2007, p. 66)

The downside to dominant expectations is that they create *blind spots*. This means that organization members risk missing small mistakes or failures, which then have a tendency to grow. According to Weick and Sutcliffe, the solution is to be aware of the dominant expectations in the organization and to constantly challenge them. This is, however, easier said than done, as we are often very lenient with ourselves in what we accept as evidence that our expectations are right. Further-more, this tendency tends to increase when we are under pressure. When we are pressed, such as in a crisis, it is normal that we fall back to our ingrained ways of thinking and behaving (Barthol & Ku, 1959). Barthol and Ku call this phenomenon *specific regression*, which means that when we are under high stress, we go back to and start to use methods and behavior that have previously been successful for us.

Specific regression occurred in firemen in a 1949 forest fire in Mann Gulch, Montana. Mann Gulch is a deep valley, wherein the fire started in a ravine. *Smokejumpers*, or firefighters who parachute into the ter-rain, fought the fire; 15 jumped down, and after just a few hours 12 of them had died. Weick (1993, p. 634) has studied this accident, and he argues that the firemen died because they did not follow chief fire-man Dodge's orders to "drop your tools" and come back out of the fire. According to Weick, these orders go completely against the firemen's education, which had taught them to always have control over their tools. Weick further argues that their tools are closely tied into their identity as firemen; had they dropped the tools, they would have been laymen, which did not feel right when they found themselves in the middle of a forest fire. He argues that it is possible that the firemen interpreted Dodge's order to mean that he had lost his mind and was no longer able to think straight.

It is also very unlikely that we will be creative in these situations, but it is, instead, much more likely that we will look for information that confirms our behavior and our expectations as correct. We will casually dismiss any other information that does not confirm our own expectations as irrelevant. Our tendency to interpret new information in a way that confirms our preconceived expectations is a challenge when considering both discovery and learning in crisis situations (Weick & Sutcliffe, 2007).

Interpretation of information

Interpreting information is a huge challenge in this context. Research (e.g., Sutcliffe, 2001) shows that leadership groups have a tendency to be skeptical about negative information and to embrace positive infor-mation that confirms their decisions. *Mindlessness* is a further prob-lem that involves organization members following rules of thumb and tried-and-true recipes, using old categories to describe and explain what they see and reacting automatically without reflection (Weick & Sutcliffe, 2007). This way of working grants organization members safety and allows them to work quickly and effectively. Everything that happens is interpreted according to the old, well-known categories, and problems are solved in the same way that they previously have been done. The problem with mindlessness is that it makes it hard to see new problems that arise, which, in turn, become worse than they would have, had they been discovered earlier. An alternative attitude is *mindfulness*, which means that organization members continuously try to refine and develop their conceptions and categories, and are therefore able to see and understand more. This also gives them a bet-ter chance to act and react in various situations. Weick et al. (1999) posit that collective mindfulness stops working if organization members do not have room to make changes and their "unusable" observations of mistakes and accidents risk being ignored or dismissed by leadership. This leads to mistakes being missed, which, in turn, increases the risk of a crisis. For this reason, Weick et al. conclude that the level of mind-fulness in an organization is determined by the level of courses of action that organization members have.

Crises and organizational learning

Learning is unavoidable (Weick & Sutcliffe, 2007). This is just as true for individuals as it is for organizations. An organization, which is made up of social relationships between individuals who work towards a certain goal, cannot avoid learning. Learning will always happen, whether we want it to or not. Nicolini and Meznar (1995, p. 738) state that "learning is a continuous process which is inherent in the very being of organizations." Everything that human beings do, including their work, is connected to learning (Brown & Duguid, 1991); by doing or being a part of something, we are also taking part in learning. In the world of schools and workplaces, it has most often been assumed that learning takes place under certain conditions, usually a specified time and place, but this is simply not true. Learning takes place in all situa-tions and thus takes place before, during and after a crisis. However, the knowledge that is gained in each crisis phase is different.

In this chapter, we primarily emphasize the learning that takes place after the crisis, as organization members have good reason to reflect on what has happened. When talking about crises, organiza-tional learning means both *creating* new knowledge and *spreading* that knowledge in the organization so that new mistakes and crisis can be avoided in the future.

A crisis is a good opportunity to learn. Weick describes crises as *cosmo-logic episodes* during which all previous notions and beliefs are uprooted and questioned (see Chapter 2, page 32). *The only way to recover from a cosmologic episode is to undergo intense organizational learning.* Those involved in crises usually experience them as deeply shaking and thus find themselves looking to understand what happened. We do not want to experience the same uncomfortable, unpleasant situation again. This drives us to try to learn in order to avoid repetition.

Early research and the traditional approach

Cyert and March (1963) began to note the phenomenon of organi-zational learning in the early 1960s. They were interested in organiza-tions' adaptability to changes in the environment and how learning related to adaptation was turned into standardized action- and decision-making rules. These were then made available to co-workers who could utilize them to solve problems in similar situations. At this point in time, researchers saw organizations as information systems, focusing on how information was handled and decisions were made.

If you go through the research on organizational learning, you will be able to identify two different approaches: the traditional and the sociocultural approach. In Heide's (2002) dissertation, he describes what characterizes the traditional approach to organizational learning:

- learning is viewed as something that can lead to improving effectiveness or development of operations;
- learning is associated with positive results such as innovation and effectiveness;
- learning is seen as something that is possible to plan, engineer and control by the leadership;
- organizational memory is presumed to exist, and it is seen as a reservoir that can be topped-up with more knowledge;
- it is assumed that learning has happened when visible changes or actions have been set in place;
- learning is said to happen separately from other organizational activities; and
- the incentives for organizational learning come from the organization's environment.

Researchers in the traditional perspective acquire theories from a behaviorist and cognitive perspective on learning and use these theories in an organizational context. These theories, however, are developed for individual psychology, and the researchers are therefore presuming that organizations learn the same way as individuals do. Many researchers have criticized this presumption, not least those who follow the social constructionist tradition.

Sociocultural perspective on organizational learning

Researchers who follow the sociocultural perspective on organizational learning emphasize that learning is not something that management can control or decide upon. Rather, learning is a natural part of all social systems. Although researchers point out that learning cannot be controlled, they argue that leaders are able to support organizational learning by highlighting, rewarding and providing the necessary conditions (time and space) for learning to occur.

The importance of dialogue for organizational learning is emphasized in the sociocultural perspective. Dialogue is fundamentally important both in the emergence of new knowledge and for the dissemination of knowledge within the organization. The close relationship between communication and knowledge can actually be found in the word *dialogue*: it comes from the Greek *dialogos*, which means that the common (*dia*) creates knowledge (*logos*). Even if learning is not the target of most conversation, it is an important side effect. Consequently, if individuals in an organization are silent, no learning will occur, and individual learning cannot be transformed into collective learning (Weick & Ashford, 2001).

Talking to others creates new understandings and insights, which, in turn, can generate new knowledge. Conversation introduces us to other people's opinions, points of view and experiences and therefore gives us the chance to reflect on our own viewpoints and perceptions, and thus develop our own knowledge. In this context, creativity is crucial for organizational members to be able to think outside the box and perceive things outside of their normal interpretive frames. The well-known American psychologist Jerome Bruner (1983, p. 183) describes creativity as "figuring out how to use what you already know in order to go beyond what you currently think."

A challenge for organizational learning is that it is, in principle, impossible to see when learning takes place (Brown & Starkey, 2000). Learning is also closely linked to identity. Brown and Starkey argue that when individuals and organizations are engaged in learning, they handle information and knowledge quite conservatively in order to maintain their self-image and identity. This means that information that threatens to change self-esteem risks being ignored, rejected, interpreted, hidden or forgotten. The recipe to counter this human process is, according to Brown and Starkey, a continuous, conscious and critically reviewing organizational identity. In other words, it is *self-reflexivity* that characterizes wise individuals and organizations, as previously mentioned in this chapter. Brown and Starkey go so far as to say that if an organization wants to develop and learn, then organizational members' common perceptions of the organization's self-image need to change.

Unlike the traditional perspective, from the sociocultural perspective, researchers emphasize that learning is always linked to a particular situation. Knowledge is rarely universal, but instead, it arises in certain situations to which it is applicable. This means that knowledge is something local, temporary and situationally dependent (Hernes & Irgens, 2012).

Organizational learning is seen in the sociocultural perspective as a natural and inevitable process that continually creates common insights, knowledge and other mental images. These affect how both individuals and groups of individuals think and act. In other words, organizational learning is an *activity* or process that occurs within a group in a particular situation.

> [O]rganizational learning is a capacity possessed not only by individual members, but by the aggregate itself. Language, action routines and material artifacts are both the means to produce and share meanings and the resource from which further cultural artifacts are created.
>
> – Weick and Westley (1996, p. 446)

In line with this, it can be seen that learning and knowledge are about people's understanding and sensemaking, and thus, it is almost impossible to orchestrate or control organizational learning. In order to understand and learn something, we first need to make sense of it – it needs to be understandable to us. As mentioned earlier, dialogue is important for learning and, of course, also for sensemaking. Stories are closely connected to dialogue; they are an important form of communication central to both sensemaking and learning (see Chapter 3). We experience and understand by telling stories for others and ourselves. When we tell stories, we construct a certain image of what has happened, and through this, filtering – either conscious or unconscious – occurs. It can even be said that without a story, which gives an event opinion and purpose, then there is nothing to be remembered (Galpin & Sims, 1999). Stories have a particularly high value in ambiguous and complex situations, such as a crisis, where there are particularly high demands on sensemaking. Aside from creating meaning and knowledge, stories help to increase collective knowledge in an organization. The stories that circulate around an organization contain knowledge that is available for the organization members

(Orr, 1996), which is spread through the constant dissemination of stories by organization members. A number of researchers, such as Boje (1994), argue that it is stories that create organizational learning and carry organization memories. Weick (1987) emphasizes that stories, narratives and narrators are essential parts of an organization, especially concerning risk and crisis management. According to Weick, in an organization that values stories and narrators, the organization members know more about their own organization, and the potential mistakes that can occur, and they have higher confidence in their abilities to manage mistakes as they know that others have successfully managed similar mistakes and that the organization is therefore more capable of crisis management.

The term *knowledge management* was penned in the 1990s, and it quickly became popular among organizational leaders. This is because, despite all the research, there is a widespread belief that it is possible to control organization member's knowledge and learning, and to thus achieve higher organizational efficiency. In the article "Odd Couple: Making Sense of the Curious Concept of Knowledge Management" Alvesson and Kärreman (2001) argue that there is a contradiction between knowledge and management and that knowledge management should be seen mostly as a way of trying to control people and information, instead of a way of facilitating and promoting knowledge production.

Crises and learning

There is not a whole lot of research on crisis and learning (Deverell, 2009, 2010). Even though crises present good opportunities for learning, it is not certain that the organization, as a whole, will learn from a crisis. It is also unclear what is learned. This is established by a number of different researchers (e.g., Boin, McConnell, & 't Hart, 2008; Smith & Elliott, 2007). There are even researchers who argue that whether crises trigger or prevent learning and development is an open question (Boin et al., 2005).

There is one perspective that dominates in both research and practice (see Chapter 2, the narrow, information-oriented perspective, pp. 29–31), in other words that crises are presumed to come from outside, and that they need to be solved so that organizations can return to normal and reach an equilibrium. An analogy can thus be drawn with thermoregulation, that body temperature is automatically controlled so that the same temperature can be retained regardless of the surrounding climate. If this is the viewpoint that dominates an orga-nization, then learning will be limited to so-called *single-loop learning*, where the focus lies on finding missing parts and correcting them so that the organization can continue working toward its goal (Argyris & Schön, 1978). Single-loop learning is usually explained with the meta-phor of a thermostat. A thermostat adapts to weather conditions and turns the heating on or off depending on whether it is hot or cold out. This means that single-loop learning takes place in an organization after some sort of adaptation to the current situation. For example, there may be a crisis regarding staff dissatisfaction about how lead-ership manages operations. If leadership acts to reduce this dissatis-faction, then single-loop learning is taking place. Organizations have, generally speaking, a hard time relearning and learning new ways to think and act, or *double-loop learning*, as doing so means questioning one's basic beliefs. Double-loop learning entails, in addition to adjust-ing behavior, reflecting on collective norms and values that govern organizational actions. When norms and values have been questioned and new alternatives have been developed, then it can be said that organizational learning has occurred. Double-loop learning is thus a profound form of learning and not just an adaptation to a current situ-ation, as is the case with single-loop learning. Other terms for double-loop learning in the literature are *meta-level learning* (Hedberg, 1981) and *generative learning* (Senge, 1990). Going back to the thermostat metaphor, double-loop learning happens if ambitions for when and why the temperature should change are questioned.

Obstacles for learning

Learning is a term that is connected to something positive. Most of us want to understand more; gain new perspectives, insights and knowl-edge; and through this develop.

> Learning is a golden concept: everybody is for it.
> – Wildavsky (1988, p. 245)

The research on the post-crisis phase contains many descriptions of how crises lead to rational values, wise insights and organizational development that, in its turn, will improve future crisis preparedness

and management (Drennan, McConnell, & Stark, 2014). Consequently, learning is linked to the concept of having a new, safer and
better future. However, there are many obstacles to learning in an
organization.

Neurotic learning is one such obstacle, in other words, that organizational members act in accordance with old norms: "this is what we've
always done and it has worked well." Even though something is true,
it is not necessary that the rule will apply every time. However, the
human desire to follow rules and principles is deceptive, as it puts us
at risk of losing sight of alternative solutions and changing ourselves
(Holt & Cornelissen, 2014). Unlearning is needed in order to prevent
this from happening (see more page 116).

Another obstacle for organizational learning is *vicarious learning*, which is a belief that organizations can control their environment and thereby create order and control. This, in turn, builds
overconfidence in the rationality of people and organizations.
Weick (1987, 1988) describes NASA before the *Challenger* accident
(see Chapter 1, page 25) as an organization with a high degree of
confidence in causality and control. There was a widespread belief
in the organization that, so long as everyone followed the usual
rules and procedures, no accidents or crises would take place. This
meant that it was impossible to predict the factors that lead to the
Challenger accident.

Often, *sociopolitical barriers* within an organization obstruct organizational learning, which also can lead to a crisis. For example, when
managers at different hierarchical levels make different decisions, such
as if the economic, technical, managerial and communicative aspects
of an organization are not united this can create blind spots, which, in
turn, lead to mistakes. Another sociopolitical barrier can, for example,
be an organizational culture of "eliminate mistakes" or "we are a flaw-
less organization" (Weick, 1993, 1996). The problem here, according to
Argyris (1977), is that this culture creates a system wherein organization members spend a lot of energy on trying to hide their mistakes.
Over time, this way of working is perceived as normal, and it causes
co-workers to have a harder time seeing and discovering their own
mistakes.

In a number of organizations, there is an *institutionalized incom-
petency to learn*, which makes learning difficult or even entirely
impossible. This is based on the double-bind situation that exists

in many organizations. According to Hennestad (1990), members of the organization are often exposed to conflicting messages from management, and it is more or less impossible for them to judge exactly what the message actually is. Hennestad emphasizes that what makes conflicting messages into a double bind is that it can neither be commented on nor discussed. For example, a manager may inform the co-workers that certain decisions are delegated to them (i.e., that they are allowed to make decisions), but that manager ultimately controls and makes the decisions regardless. In this case, the co-worker cannot comment on the situation if he or she believes that management will punish him or her. In other words, the double bind contributes to a lack of meta-communication, that is, communication about communication, which, in turn, makes organizational learning harder.

Decision-makers' and groups' *ego* is another obstacle for organizational learning. Pauchant and Mitroff (1992) posit that vulnerable organizations are unable to think and feel that the world is different from themselves. In these organizations, there is often a belief that all parties like the organization. These organizations also have a strong tendency to ignore, dismiss, reinterpret, hide or misplace information that threatens their ego.

In sum, if organizations are going to be able to learn from crises, they need to let go of the idea that everything can be controlled and arranged and, instead, plan for and prepare themselves for surprises. Organizations that do not make room for reflection effectively give space for *functional stupidity* to develop (Alvesson & Spicer, 2012). According to Alvesson and Spicer, functional stupidity exists in organizations where the intellectual capacity of organizational members is not fully used. This, in turn, leads to "*stupidity management*," which exempts or ignores any doubts about how things are being done. This lays the foundation for negative upward information to be minimized and for solely positive information to reach the leadership. This also creates a sense of security in the organization's choices and interpretations. In other words, any doubts, reflections and dialogue that would make the organization more open for alternative perspectives, which, in turn, would make the organization more capable of handling the complex and ever-changing world, are thrown out. In order to be able to develop and produce new knowledge, an organization needs to be able to question existing frames, stories and concepts (Barton et al., 2015).

Obstacles for organizational learning

- Incapacity to spread upward negative information
- "No bad news" culture
- Neurotic learning
- Vicarious learning
- Sociopolitical barriers
- Decision-makers' ego

Weick and Sutcliffe (2007) say that we need to trust our gut feeling to a much greater extent. When we feel surprised, hazy or insecure, when we feel that something is wrong but cannot put our finger on it, we need to hold onto that feeling. We need to resist the human tendency to smooth over the situation and interpret it as normal, and the longer time we let the situation continue without reacting, the greater the risk that we will interpret it as normal. According to Weick and Sutcliffe, in order to avoid the normalizing process, we need to *anomalize*, that is to say, be aware of this process, and put our attention on any deviations that occur. The challenge is to proactively work to make organization members pay attention to deviations and report them and to not be tempted to quickly categorize events into known categories. This can happen, for example, when groups discuss deviations and mistakes and try to collectively find patterns. Managers at different levels should be responsible for ensuring that these processes are in place.

Both time and energy are required for reflection, but this runs in contrast with normal operations. Because most operations are characterized by a high tempo, there is a risk that reflection and learning will be culled. This usually happens in organizations where reflection and learning are not on the agenda and are not considered to be important or worthwhile. Because of this, it is especially important that someone in the organization is responsible for ensuring that continuous reflection and learning are considered important and take place.

The art of working with resilience and learning

- Managers need to first understand the importance of reflection and learning

- Managers need to set a good example
- Create room for and encourage reflection dialogues
- Give attention and reward
- Normalize

When we do things correctly, we don't actually learn anything new but only confirm our own success. It has long been known that organizations that have been successful for a long time have a poorer ability to absorb and respond to negative information. On the other hand, organizations that have gone through a crisis are more sensitive and more quickly adapt and respond to change. Thus, it is often difficult for organizations to learn from their experiences: the feedback that organization members get is usually interpreted within the framework of the organization's dominant culture, and at other times, weak signals for negative change are not detected.

Gilpin and Murphy (2008) describe the well-known Enron crisis case as an example of an organization which failed to address negative information. Enron was an international US energy company that, when at the time it went bankrupt in 2001, was a world leader in its field and had more than 20,000 co-workers. The company generated huge profits and was applauded year after year as one of the best and most innovative organizations in its field. It was also popular with investors, but its reputation was stained when the company was accused of both cartel formation and misconduct in its foreign affairs. However, illegal consolidated bookkeeping, wherein costs and debts were eliminated through advanced planning, is what ultimately led to Enron's demise. Enron was able to show strong profits even when its operations were in the red. This led to the US security trading authority, the Securities and Exchange Commission, reviewing Enron's bookkeeping, and stock prices fell. At the same time, insider trading was going on, and people with knowledge about what was going on in the company sold their shares before the information reached the market. At the end of 2001, Enron's management applied for bankruptcy.

In Enron, as in many other organizations, a *"no bad news" culture* was prevalent, wherein all negative information was pushed aside and ignored. Such a culture holds the risk of quickly leading to self-censorship and self-persuasion that the organization has chosen and done the right thing. Within Enron there was a strong perception that its business model was outstanding as it created success and innovation; this was perhaps enhanced by all the positive attention the company received from the mass media. All information that did not confirm that this was the case was completely ignored. This can be linked to the idiom: "nothing fails like success." Weick (1993) stresses that both *extreme self-confidence*, which characterized, for example, Enron, and the opposing *extreme uncertainty* create poor conditions for organizational learning. These two states prevent what organizations need most in changing situations, namely *curiosity*, *openness* and *high sensitivity*. Weick believes that wise organizations, which avoid the extremes, have the greatest chance at improving their adaptability.

> It is within the abnormal that the habitual struggles and becomes open to view.
>
> – Weick (1993, p. 633)

Emergent learning strategies

Organizational learning during and after a crisis should lead to changes both in behavior and in cognitive understandings, or how things are understood. Gilpin and Murphy (2008) point out that organizational crises require a combination of emergent learning and reflection, as these situations are critical occasions during which culture, goals and relationships to different audiences can be reevaluated. *Emergent learning strategies* mean stressing the individual co-worker's responsibility to be proactive, to be reflexive and to constantly try to develop knowledge (Megginson, 1996). In other words, this strategy is linked to the sociocultural perspective of learning, emphasizing that learning is linked to a particular sociocultural environment and is about sensemaking and understanding. This strategy can be placed in contrast to the traditional planning strategy, where the emphasis lies on leadership and management creating the conditions for and controlling learning.

> Most executives understand that tougher competition will require more effective *learning*, broader empowerment and greater commitment from everyone in the company. Moreover,

they understand that the key to better performance is better *communication*. For 20 years or more, business leaders have used a score of *communication* tools – focus groups, organizational surveys, management-by-walking-around and others – to convey and to gather the information needed to bring about change.

What is new is that these familiar techniques, used correctly, will actually inhibit the *learning* and *communication* that twenty-first-century corporations will require not just of managers but of every co-worker.

– Argyris (1994, p. 77)

Co-workers are central to successful crisis management. Learning in crises does not occur when co-workers consult books, but instead when they create new skills through improvisation (see below) to overcome the obstacles they encounter. Once again, sensemaking is crucial to people's ability to understand, act and learn. Sensemaking occurs after a crisis, that is to say, the organization members construct a certain picture and understanding of what has happened, and this generates new knowledge.

Three types of learning post-crisis

According to the crisis communications researchers Seeger et al. (2003), there are three types of organizational learning post-crisis:

• *Retrospective sensemaking:* Once the intense crisis phase has passed, space for reflection and understanding opens. In the post-crisis phase, organization members try to understand what has happened. As with all sensemaking processes, understanding and meaning can only arise *after* we have participated in something. In other words, sensemaking takes place retrospectively. Seeger et al. emphasize that post-crisis communication not only serves as a public apology, but the explanations given are even an opportunity to increase the internal understanding of what happened and why the organization responded in a certain way. This creates new knowledge that can be used to prevent or reduce the risk of a corresponding crisis situation recurring.

- *Reconsidering structures:* Over time, both formal and informal structures arise in all organizations, for example, who is responsible for what and who is allowed to decide certain issues. These structures are rarely questioned. Some sort of disruption is needed in order to question the taken-for-granted structures (see double-loop learning). Crises are such a disruption, giving an opportunity for reflection and questioning. Crises are further, in line with the Chinese definition of crises, also an opportunity for development (see Chapter 1, p. 13). Researchers like Huber (1991) argue that organizations need to "unlearn" in order to question their structures. Through unlearning, opportunities for learning are created. The changes that occur may be small, such as increased crisis awareness, but oftentimes they are much deeper, such as new leadership or ways of working in the organization.

- *Proxy learning:* In many organizations, learning occurs when both leadership and general organization members follow other organization's crises, not least through the intense media coverage that usually goes on. Institutional theory has taught us that organizations mimic other organization's behavior and therefore do not need to themselves develop knowledge in order to be successful.

? **Questions for discussion**

Imagine that you work as a manager at a construction company where there has recently been a workplace accident in which two co-workers were seriously injured. The accident has received a lot of attention in the media, where complaints about leadership having turned a blind eye to a worsening workplace environment and increased stress levels among co-workers for a long time have been published. It has also come out that the company had no plans or systematic work to avoid accidents.

You and your fellow managers are going to meet to discuss what is important to learn from the crisis and how you are going to work in the future. Think back to what was written in this chapter and write down five points that you would want to take with you to the meeting with leadership.

Chapter 7

What can we learn, and how?

IN THIS LAST chapter we summarize and discuss the lessons from the previous chapters. The first section of this chapter deals with the development of crisis communication as a research field. We then move on to the second section, where we focus on the strong myth that organizations are rational units that can orchestrate and control development. Against this, we place a clear trend in organizational research, focusing on the importance of accepting and understanding the importance of the random, and of improvisation. Organizations and their environment are complex, and this cannot be ignored. We need to embrace complexity and realize that it gives rise to paradoxes, which we need to acknowledge and relate to. This insight is important for how we look at and handle internal crisis communication. The chapter concludes by presenting a number of practical tips on how to act in terms of internal communication before, during and after a crisis.

Crisis communication – a research field in flux

In recent years, crisis communication has grown from a specific area within public relations to one of the dominant topics within public relations research. Crisis communication is even closely related to three other main fields within public relations:

- Issues management – a strategic analysis of the outside world in order to detect trends and changes that can develop into an "issue," that is, a matter that attracts the attention of stakeholders and potentially will lead to a crisis for the organization.

- Risk communication.
- Reputation management (Coombs, 2010).

As we discussed at the beginning of this book, public relations research has been mainly interested in external communication, and this also runs true for crisis communication. The research on crisis communication has also been characterized by an emphasis on communication after the crisis has broken out. A key research area here has been the organization's response strategies, and how the organization's image can be preserved or repaired (see Chapter 2). In recent years, however, more and more researchers have argued that crisis management and crisis communication are about much more than the response after a crisis has arisen. The post-crisis phase has gained an increasing role in research on crisis communication. At the same time, more and more researchers are saying that even internal communication needs to be emphasized if we are going to be better at avoiding, managing and learning from crisis. A third developing trend is that crises are increasingly seen as a natural part of an organization's existence, that is to say, crises are being normalized (Vigsø, 2015).

These shifts raise new questions about the boundaries of the research field and what kind of theoretical perspectives are relevant to the study of crisis communication. According to Vigsø (2015), the interest in what happens before and after a crisis can be interpreted as though two thirds of crisis communication is not directly connected to the crisis. What, then, is crisis communication? When presenting the results from our study on the university hospital – where we, among other things, experience the co-worker's experiences of major organizational changes as a crisis, and how deviation management can be seen as an example of crisis avoidance – we have sometimes been asked whether this really is crisis communication research, or if it is more organizational communication in a broader sense. We argue, however, that one's perspective is crucial to whether something is counted as crisis research. Error management can, for example, be studied from a number of different perspectives, for example, patient safety, organizational learning, risk management or as a way of discovering weak signals that can develop into a crisis (see Simonsson & Heide, 2018). Vigsø (2015) is in the same school of thought and argues that crisis communications research needs to develop a more holistic view of an organization's communications and see them as "multifunctional," that is, that one communication activity can serve several purposes.

Some may see the development toward a broader perspective as a threat to crisis communication as an independent research field. We argue, however, that it is rather the opposite – this development is necessary to take crisis communications research a step further. As there is now also an increased focus on internal processes, it is also necessary to not only get theoretical sustenance from within public relations research but to also get acquainted with the research on organizational communication – which we have tried to do in this book. Roux-Dufort (2007) claims that crisis researchers have been too focused on exceptional and abnormal events. The more critical or serious an event is, the more legitimate and important it has been to study the event. This means that crisis research has contributed to the knowledge about how to handle exceptional situations such as accidents and natural disasters but not much to the knowledge about how organizations work and can develop. Roux-Dufort (2007) believes that the emphasis on the crisis itself needs to be balanced with an analysis of the organization in which the crisis occurs, or the organizations involved in the crisis. Crises are often created by the organizations themselves, and we need to go beyond the actual crisis event to thoroughly understand how the crisis was constructed.

Both-thinking

There is a long-standing myth, among both practitioners and researchers, that organizations are rational units that can, with access to enough information, make optimal decisions, plan, go through with plans and produce certain results. In Chapter 5 (see page 76) we mentioned the rational man myth that Simon discussed at the end of the 1950s. Simon (1957) developed the decision-making theory *bounded rationality* and argued that people can only be boundedly rational, as they are incapable of processing all the available information. Moreover, as we mentioned in the same chapter, Brunsson (1982) has written much on how organizations do not function rationally when making decisions. Weick (1995) questioned the myth of the rational organization during his entire career, as this myth misses the interpretive aspect of information. Weick emphasizes the definition of sensemaking, that is to say, we people always make sense of information from our own interpretive frames. As the world is socially constructed, we, argues Weick, will never find the truth, as it simply does not exist. When making decisions in complex situations we need to create a certain meaning that helps us to understand the situation, and therefore enables us to act.

In recent years, researchers have been increasingly interested in the *nonrational* in organizations, such as the importance of improvisation to success in crises, and the importance of *serendipity*, or an organization's ability to succeed due to chance. Serendipity in this case means the *chance discoveries of something that subsequently proves to be valuable to the organization*. In other words, serendipity is linked to luck (Cunha, Rego, Clegg, & Lindsay, 2015). This runs in contrast to the traditional understanding of organizations as a rational system in which control and order are key. In reality, all organizations have elements of both order and chaos (Brown & Eisenhardt, 1997), meaning that organizations must both seek and attain a certain level of order and control, but there need to also be openings for new opportunities or situations that have not been previously seen or agreed on. If too much energy is placed on trying to control, plan and manage, the organization will not be able to respond to the unforeseen, transient situations that arise. Organizational leadership needs to also actively search for and listen to co-worker information and knowledge in order to not miss out on important opportunities (Day & Schoemaker, 2008; Hassan, 2011). A prerequisite for better handling our complex and fast-changing world is that among the members of the organization *there is an awareness that the organization cannot plan for everything.* The co-workers therefore need to have an attitude that improvisation is good and that they should not blindly believe in and follow plans and detail management. Subsequently, co-workers need to have sufficient decision-making powers to be able to actually make decisions.

Managing unexpected events

The literature notes two ways that organizations manage unexpected events:

a   Meeting the surprises through *preparation*
b   Knowingly *exposing* organizations to new and unusual situations (Cunha et al., 2015)

The nature of unexpected events and serendipity is that they cannot be orchestrated and controlled. However, organizations in which the organization members are well versed in different areas of specialization are mentally well prepared to act when the unexpected occurs. These specialist skills bring with them better opportunities to perceive and adapt the organization to the unexpected.

The second way of managing the unexpected assumes that it is possible to prepare to act when in foreign situations or when the unexpected occurs. An organization can do this by constantly confronting new situations and by challenging its own assumptions and entering into new business areas that contain both risks and opportunities (see double-loop learning in Chapter 6, page 109).

Cuhna et al. come to the conclusion that leaders can create good capabilities for organizations to manage the unexpected by fostering and embracing the unknown and unexpected and by seeing these as important opportunities for discovery and challenge. It is also important that the organization has an atmosphere wherein the co-workers feel safe to fail and ensures that their skills are sufficient for coping with the unexpected.

Knudsen and Lemmergaard (2014) have penned the term *strategic serendipity*, meaning that organizations as a communicative actor strategically exploit the benefits of other actors in, for example, a crisis. This is especially true in crisis situations where external actors act and communicate different messages through social media; in this case, there is a great need to act quickly based on the situation. In such a situation, *improvisation* is necessary for communication professionals, who need to work strategically instead of just being senders in a simple communications process (Eriksson, 2009). Our experience is that all modern research in crisis communication is pointing precisely in this direction. Organizations can never have full control over their communications, but they can enable and support by creating frameworks and platforms for communication.

Improvisation

Improvisation is a word that often draws up images of painters and artists – improvisational art, improvisational theater and improvisational jazz. That is to say, we usually connect improvisation with creativity and innovation. But even in many other situations, improvisation is obviously present. It is something that most of us exercise daily. Cunha et al. argue that the traditional and individual-focus view of improvisation, as a normal anticipation, ignores or tones down the importance of an organization's resources, power and politics (Cunha, Clegg, Rego, & Neves, 2014). Today, improvisation is seen as an *important organizational capacity*, which is especially important given the complex and ever-changing world. However, as organizations are constructed for order, control and predictability, they therefore try to avoid uncertainty, which means that improvisation is easier said than done (Cunha et al., 2014). It can therefore be said that organizations need leadership that understands the importance of improvisation and that talks about and highlights successful examples of improvised solutions to problems.

Trial and error are some of the most basic forms of improvisation. Simply put, trial and error involve trying and bringing forward different methods and seeing which one is the most successful. As mentioned earlier, plans can be obstructed during a crisis, and organizational leadership needs to trust in their co-workers' competencies and opinions. Improvisation and adaptation are often the best solutions in these situations. This can be called *ad hoc improvisation*, which happens when the unexpected occurs (Cunha et al., 2014). While the result of improvisation is naturally not always successful, the organization has in any case acted.

Solid creativity is a prerequisite for all forms of improvisation. An individual who only has basic knowledge in an area has difficulty improvising. The newly graduated teacher adheres strictly to his or her lesson plan, the young lover adheres strictly to the tips he has received about the noble art of loving and the inexperienced chef follows their recipes from A to Z. Once people have gained more experience in their area through practice, conversations with others and further education and reading, they become more capable of improvising. By producing crisis plans involving crisis management and communications, organizations create the necessary knowledge for crisis management. In spite of this, organizations generally spend too little time practicing crisis situations, which would create better crisis awareness amongst organization members and increase their knowledge.

Paradoxical tensions

In an article published in the research journal *Public Relations Inquiry* we present five different paradoxical tensions found at the university hospital we studied, but that can also be expected to be present in other organizations (Heide & Simonsson, 2015). The point of the paradoxical tensions is that the two opposite ends of the paradoxes both simultaneously exist in the organization. There is, however, a clear tendency for one of the positions to dominate and to be the starting point when making decisions.

The five paradoxical tensions that we identified are the following:

- Episodic–emerging
- Centralized–decentralized
- Professional–organizational
- Planning–improvisation
- External–internal

The first paradox deals with the tension between two different views on crises. In the episodic view, crises are seen as big events that threaten the organization's central operations and existence. In other words, this perspective represents the functionalist view on crises, and it is assumed that crises can be managed with proper planning, preparations and resources. In the hospital we also found another, opposing view on crises, namely, as something emergent, slowly developing into a bigger crisis. From this perspective, it is assumed that before a crisis there are a lot of signals of error and deviations that can be detected, thus enabling the organization to avoid a major crisis. People's perceptions are emphasized in the emerging view on crises, as these perceptions are crucial to whether an event is viewed as a crisis and how it is handled. The second tension relates to the organization's structure, leadership and communication. The university hospital is, on one hand, a rather centralized and hierarchically structured organization, but on the other hand, there are also divisions and units within the organization that are loosely linked and decentralized. For example, daily work in the emergency room is practically independent of other departments, and different departments within the hospital often informally collaborate. We noted, however, that the traditional, hierarchical organizational principle tends to prevail in crisis management. The third tension relates to the two different logics that exist in the organization – the medical and the administrative. In a professional organization such as the hospital, the "professional" logic tends to dominate. Professional in this context means the occupational groups who are specialists within the core area of the business (i.e., doctors and nurses). When considering crisis management and crisis communication, the third tension implies that the medical logic overshadows the administrative, which means that the focus lies on medical crises. The fourth tension addresses the question of planning versus improvisation in crisis management. Again, we found both approaches within the organization; however, the traditional overconfidence in planning, prediction and control dominated. Finally, the fifth tension relates to whether crisis communication is primarily oriented toward internal or external groups. At the university hospital, as in many other organizations, external communication was prioritized. Several of our interviewees stated that they looked to the external mass media, such as daily newspapers and social media, to get information during a crisis.

The question is then how practitioners should manage these organizational paradoxes. The existence of these paradoxes in most organizations makes balancing them a challenge for both managers and other co-workers. Lewis (2000, p. 764) has conducted a literature review and found that there are three mutually related ways to cope with these tensions:

- Acceptance
- Confrontation
- Transcendence

As we said in Chapter 5 (see page 75), acceptance is an important part of us humans being able to handle crises, no matter what they are (see Kåver, 2004). Acceptance does not necessarily mean that we like the situation, but we accept it as it is. This is important for us to be able to act appropriately based on the current situation. According to Breit (2014), acceptance means embracing and learning to live with paradoxes, meaning that you are aware of them and do not try to ignore them. Confrontation means that within an organization, you discuss the paradoxes and try to develop new ways to adapt to them. Finally, transcendence means trying to develop the capacity to think paradoxically. This requires, in turn, what Bateson (1972) calls *second-order thinking*. This involves self-reflection, wherein organizational members critically examine the assumptions that lead them to prefer one end of the paradox to the other. The purpose of transcending earlier, often taken-for-granted beliefs, is to challenge a unilateral and simplistic thinking process where paradoxes are accepted by seeing them as natural characteristics rather than counteracting them.

The three ways of dealing with paradoxical tensions that Lewis suggests are by no means easy projects. In organizations marked by managerialism (see page 30) they may be particularly difficult; there, a cultural shift is needed in order to make these changes. The thoughts Lewis has on managing organizational paradoxes are in line with the thinking in high-reliability organizations (HROs). Ultimately, organizations wishing to be successful in the long-term need to begin meta-communicating more often (Ashcraft & Trethewey, 2004; Tracey, 2002). Meta-communication means communicating about communication (Watzlawick, Beavin, & Jackson, 1967). Through meta-communication, organization members can embrace the tensions and find ways to deal with them. We suggest in our article in *Public Relations Inquiry* (Heide & Simonsson, 2015) that leaders and co-workers should discuss questions such as

- *Which paradoxical tensions related to crisis communication do we struggle with in our organization?* As we have previously noted, it is important to be aware of the problems and obstacles that face an organization. It is thus important that the management in the organization tries to chart which paradoxical tensions exist in order to be able to handle them. In other words, we need to be able to face reality before we can improve the situation. On the previous pages we have given examples of fairly common paradoxical tensions, but all organizations are unique, and there are, of course, many tensions that you can identify.

- *Which tensions are the most important for us to confront and transcend?* Once the organization has an overview of the major paradoxical tensions, the next step is to prioritize which tensions are most pressing to deal with first. In the case of the university hospital, we felt that the first tension, episodic–emerging, was most important. This tension relates to how the organization views crisis and has the greatest significance for crisis management and internal crisis communication

- *Each paradoxical tension consists of a continuum with opposed poles – where on that continuum would we place our current way of working with internal crisis communication? And where on the continuum would it be most optimal for us to be?* This is obviously not an easy task, but the important thing about this exercise is the process itself. By identifying problems, increasing awareness and discussing, you are setting yourself on the right path to improve internal crisis communications.

• *Why is one pole of the paradoxical tension favored over another – which underlying assumptions have led us to that?* This question is related to Lewis's third suggestion on how organizations should handle paradoxical tensions–transcendence. One way to handle it is to discuss what we measure and reward within the organization. Another important question is what groups and professions are associated with status. It was clear that at the university hospital the doctors and their medical logic had the highest status, which was reflected in what was viewed as a crisis and how it should be handled and communicated.

• *How can we integrate and benefit from including both poles in the tension?* One of the paradoxical tensions we identified at the university hospital was the professional–organizational. As mentioned earlier, the doctors are the strongest professional group, and their medical logic often seems to take a different course than the administrative/leadership logic. Both these logics have a justification, and it is therefore important that the logics can be utilized in a mutually beneficial manner. One condition is that representatives of the two logics meet and try to understand each other's requirements and starting points.

This means that paradoxical tensions cannot be seen as an either–or situation or that one paradox can be prioritized over another. The different tensions should be integrated into a both/and perspective (Smith & Lewis, 2011), as both poles are valid and important to the organization.

Lessons about internal communication before, during and after the crisis

The American professor in crisis communication Timothy Coombs (2010) points out that crises are unusual events that cannot be predicted, yet they can be regarded as expected. Sooner or later, most organizations end up in a crisis situation, and crisis management should be an integral part of all organizations' business development. In the following sections we summarize a number of lessons that are relevant to the internal aspects of an organization's crisis management. These lessons can hardly be used as a simple recipe, but rather should be seen as a number of issues or aspects to which each organization should relate. The lessons are sorted into the three different phases of a crisis.

Pre-crisis

In the first section, we present advice on what is important to think about in order to avoid and prepare oneself for a crisis.

- *Clarify the goals of internal crisis communication:* A first step in creating good internal crisis communication is to discuss what you want to achieve with internal communication in connection with crises. Without clear goals, there is no compass with which to lead the communications, and thus, you will probably work from different pictures of what you want to prioritize and how the communication should be. In Chapter 3, we proposed four goals for internal crisis communication: provide instructions, help to process the crisis, strengthen loyalty and engagement and create organizational crisis awareness. Communications efforts linked to the last two goals are not always considered to be pure crisis communication but are, instead, closely related to how internal communication is largely managed and functioning. For example, strengthening loyalty and dedication is not only important for engaging co-workers as ambassadors in a crisis but also in order to maintain staff and motivate co-workers to be committed to the organization as a whole (see the earlier discussion about the multifunctionality of communication).

- *Make the crisis plan a living document:* We have emphasized the dangers of being overconfident in crisis plans many times in this book. The problem is that people often place too much energy on the plan as a *product* but very little energy on the communications *process* that is necessary to make a plan approved, understood and used. Bringing forward and developing a crisis plan should be done with a clear idea in mind of how the plan will be implemented. It is usually not enough to specify that it is the responsibility of each line manager to make sure that the plan is known. As manager, you have the responsibility to communicate a large number of plans and steering documents – for example, in areas such as gender equality, business plans, environmental issues and work environment. In other words, managers need support and assistance in implementing crisis plans.

- *Be sensitive to what is perceived as a crisis and discuss what different types of crises require from the organization's internal communication:* We found in our study of the hospital that the formal crisis preparedness primarily included events that could constitute direct and immediate threats to care capacity and patient safety, such as fire, bomb threats and water leakage, and it is, of course, important to be prepared for that type of event. At the same time, the interviews showed that the merger and the constant budget cutbacks had led to a situation in which some co-workers experienced that the organization, as a whole, was in crisis. From the perspective of the co-workers, there were thus other types of crises apart from those included in the formal crisis plans. Our point is not that all types of crises (see Figure 2.1 on page 37) should be included in the same plan – they are too different for that to be realistic. What is important here is to raise awareness of co-workers' perceptions of a crisis and what the different types of crisis require from internal communication. A fire requires a functioning crisis plan and the opportunity to send out fast and accurate information. When budget cutbacks and reorganization have been taking place for a long time and co-workers no longer feel that they can do their work, an organization needs crisis leaders (in opposition to managers and commanders; see Chapter 4, pp. 57 –59) wherein you continuously communicate to create good internal relations, openness, dialogue and collaboration.

- *Build trust levels among leadership, managers and co-workers:* If there is no established trust between management and co-workers, then there may arise a gap between what management intends to communicate and how the co-workers interpret the information they receive. Even ambitious and well-implemented communication efforts during a crisis can be interpreted as distanced, cold, opportunistic and irresponsible. Well-established high trust levels between different groups before the crisis can act as a sort of "vaccine" against mistrust, accusations and negative ambassadorship during the crisis itself.

- *Develop a safety culture wherein mistakes are seen as opportunities for learning*: Most crises are forewarned by a number of warning signs that something is going to happen. The ability to detect and interpret these early signals is thus an important part of a safety culture. Discovering early warning signals is closely linked to seeing mistakes as something natural, and as an opportunity to learn. A safety culture is a culture in which there are both structures (channels and forums) through which to communicate mistakes and deviations and a climate of trust in which co-workers want to and dare to talk about risk factors and mistakes. It is somewhat of a paradox that while many organizations experience an overflow of information, there is still a lack of so-called upward negative information – instead, negative or critical information stays among co-workers and does not reach managers further up in the hierarchy. Barton et al. (2015) posit that it is important for managers to constantly seek and encourage reporting and discussion of deviations. In addition, leadership has an important role in the interpretation of weak signals of change, as they guide and set the frameworks for these interpretations, by categorizing situations as safe or unsafe. Managers at all levels in an organization act as *role models*, and by clearly stating that there are seldom no definite answers or absolute interpretations of a situation, they are able to promote questioning, reflection and sensemaking among co-workers.

- *Develop channels for rapid dissemination of information*: Even before the crisis has begun, there should be a plan in place for how information can quickly and easily be sent out. Each organization has its own special conditions, and it is therefore difficult to give general tips on the safe and quick flow of information – other than saying that you should not rely on only one channel or path of information. In a geographically dispersed organization with a well-developed intranet and staff with access to their own computers, it is natural to use the intranet as the primary channel for information dissemination. Some organizations have developed a hidden website with information that is only activated during a crisis. Similarly, there may be certain parts of an intranet that are only activated during a crisis. Certain information, such as crisis management plans, should, of course, be available all the time, while other parts, such as discussion forums and Q&As can be prepared and ready for quick activation. In some organizations, where personnel do not have access to digital media, line communication or spreading information through managers at different levels, is the way to go. In this case, it is important to clarify who will be a substitute if a line manager is not present.

During the crisis

In this section we give advice about how internal crisis communication should be handled during the actual crisis. Communication in this phase of the crisis is primarily about giving instructions and informing co-workers of how they are expected to act in order to solve the crisis, but it is also important to help co-workers deal with the concerns, stress and uncertainty that often arise in a crisis situation.

- *Separate between different groups of co-workers – directly and indirectly affected:* Naturally, it is important to prioritize those co-workers who are directly involved in the crisis during the most acute phase. If, for example, there is a fire in a hospital, giving co-workers fast information on what they need to do to get themselves, patients and others to safety is of utmost importance. At the same time, you cannot forget the indirectly affected co-workers – that is to say, the co-workers in other departments that are not situated close to the fire, or that are not directly affected by it. The indirectly affected often have a number of questions such as "What is the hospital doing to resolve this situation?" "Which information has been externally communicated?" "What do my patients know when they come here?" "Can I help in any way?" and "Have any of my colleagues been injured?" Although information to ensure people's safety and health needs to be prioritized, the next step is ensuring that all co-workers – even those not directly affected – get information from their own organization. This creates security, clarity in the flow of information (there is a high risk of conflicting information and "double information" if co-workers do not know what has been said to different target groups) and increases the co-workers' incentive and capability to be calm and assured communicators toward external bodies.
- *Continuously communicate and confirm which internal channels will be used:* We can expect co-workers to actively seek information

in order to make sense of and create an understanding of what is happening and what should be done during a crisis. If senior management and managers fail to continuously inform, they will essentially create an information vacuum that will be filled with rumors, speculations or information from external sources. It is important to be clear about which channels will be used for the dissemination of information – otherwise, confusion and a number of questions will arise about that particular issue. For example, as a co-worker, can I expect to receive text messages with the most important information, or should I look for new information on the intranet? It is also important to constantly keep the co-workers informed; it is better to say that there is no new information to give than to not say anything at all. It may also be good to keep in mind that relevant information does not necessarily need to be information about a new decision or what the next step will be – it may often be the process itself. For example, if management takes several hours to discuss the current situation with the police, it is relevant to tell co-workers about this conversation instead of waiting until it is over to tell the co-workers about the result.

- *Comment on your external image internally:* Always communicate internally before you communicate externally is a golden rule to follow. Even a five-minute head start may be enough for the co-workers to feel that they are being prioritized. By allowing co-workers to hear negative or serious information from external sources first, you take the risk of diminishing loyalty or creative negative ambassadorship. Sometimes, however, you may not be able to communicate with the co-workers first. This may be due to leaks or simply not being able to compete with the speed of the external media. Journalistic organizations are in many ways built for crisis communication: they are used to a high publishing rate, they can quickly redirect and mobilize resources, they have personnel for most hours of the day and the principles for newsworthiness that largely emphasize the unexpected and dramatic are cut for a crisis. Some organizations are under very hard media coverage, and it is almost impossible for them to match the speed and scope of the external media's coverage. What these organizations can do, however, is to comment on and discuss their external image internally. If senior management and the managers (with the help of communicators) do not internally comment on their external image, they miss the chance to frame and influence the co-workers' perception of how the crisis is being handled. An absence of communication about the external image can thus be seen as a lost opportunity to exercise leadership.

- *Leaders as active sensemakers:* Providing brief and clear instructions on what to do, when to do it and by whom, is a part of communications during the acute crisis phase. Other questions that arise in a crisis are more complex and ambiguous in their nature and thus require both an explanation and an interpretation. These questions can include "What is actually happening?" "How serious is it?" "How are we, as an organization, reacting?" and "What is our answer to criticisms that we have received?" What management says and does in response to that type of question are of great importance to how co-workers actually interpret and act in a crisis situation. The management and the immediate manager often have slightly different communicative roles here. Senior managers need to provide the same overall information to all co-workers and to clarify the organization's position: how do we look at this situation, what are we doing and why? The line managers at different levels of the organization are responsible for strengthening and relating the overall information to their own operations. The immediate manager is a necessary complement to the general information communicated by senior management via different internal channels. The immediate managers should also bring their co-workers in for meetings with the opportunity for dialogue, wherein co-workers can get out their worries and feelings about the situation. Both senior management and the immediate managers should be present and visible as much as possible in order to provide support, feedback and empathy. Finally, it should be emphasized that the role of leaders as sensemakers is not merely about highlighting the positives and making their organization look as good as possible. Instead, it is often much more trustworthy to provide a picture as balanced as possible – to tell co-workers about both the successful and unsuccessful. This way, co-workers are far better equipped to respond to criticisms from external stakeholders.
- *Listen to and seek feedback from co-workers:* Some people seem to link effective crisis communication with one-way communication – providing quick, clear guidelines to co-workers about how to resolve

the crisis. However, there is much evidence that points to the importance of managers, communicators and other responsible parties
listening to and being open to feedback from their co-workers during the actual crisis. First, this shows support for the co-workers
and gives them the support they need to handle the crisis. Second,
by listening and asking for feedback, you can find out how the co-
workers interpret and respond to the information they receive.
Even in a "normal" situation, communicating and reaching out are
difficult, and these only become harder during a crisis, which is
often akin to a stressful situation. It is therefore important that you
as an employer try to find out how what you are saying is being
understood in order to know if you need to correct, amplify, tweak
or repeat the message. Third, feedback is important for making
informed decisions. Co-workers can tell you about the reactions that
they receive from customers, patients and other stakeholder groups,
which, among other things, provides a picture of which information
is missing.

- *Equip co-workers in their role as communicators:* Most of the advice
we have presented is about creating communication that facilitates
the management of the crisis itself, but the advice does also aim
to support co-workers in their communication with external stakeholders. If you as a co-worker receive ongoing information, have
the opportunity to ask questions, provide feedback about what does
not work, are able to work out your own internal concerns and
so on, then you also have the capability of responding to external
stakeholders in a competent and trustworthy manner. It is typically
advised to appoint one or more spokespersons who have received
special education in dealing with media and crisis communications
during a crisis. The idea is that the organization should have *one*
outward voice in order to create as consistent a message as possible.
As far as contact with the media is concerned, there may be a valid
point in appointing a spokesperson, but at the same time, it should
be remembered that public organizations especially are expected to
be transparent and journalists often want to speak to co-workers.
In addition, the concept of having only one voice is a little outdated
in a society where anyone can publish and spread information via
social media. Our advice is to instead see the potential in co-workers
as communicators and to give them the best possible requisites to
be able to handle that role.

Post-crisis

In the post-crisis phase, there is often still great confusion and inse-curity among the co-workers. During this phase, the organization will work to get back to some sort of "normal" wherein energy can be directed back toward everyday operations. The goal here should not necessarily be to return to how things were before the crisis. All crises are excellent opportunities for reflection, development and learning. These are the times when past truths can be torn apart and questioned. The wise and conscious organization will take crises seriously even after they have passed.

• *Continue to strengthen organizational identity:* It is fundamentally important to keep strengthening the co-workers' identification with the organization in this phase of the crisis. Most organizations typi-cally focus on *image repair* during this phase, but it is just as, if not more, important to repair organizational identity (i.e., *identity repair*). As mentioned several times before in this book, co-workers are the most important ambassadors for an organization. Depend-ing on the type of crisis that has occurred, co-workers may be filled with doubt. "Is this an organization I want to keep working for?" was probably a question many co-workers at Volkswagens (vw) asked themselves a couple of years ago. On September 18, 2015, it was found that vw, like many other car manufacturers, had not pro-vided accurate data on its diesel emissions for many years – the so-called Dieselgate. It came out that vw staff had installed *defeat devices* in their cars to trick authorities' emissions tests and give the impression that the cars released less exhaust gases than they actually did. Since 2011, co-workers had raised alarms about this, but for some reason, leadership had chosen to silence the situation. It is, accordingly, important that the organization not only tries to repair its external stakeholders' trust but that it also tries to repair co-worker trust. vw immediately started campaigns to try to restore trust in external stakeholders. Both Audi and vw owners received apology letters from the top management, and whole-page adver-tisements with apologies have been published in both morning and evening newspapers. We do not have any insight into the internal communication in vw during this time period, but we would not be surprised if much more focus was devoted to the external image repair rather than to identity repair.

- *Accept ambiguity and be open to other options:* When trying to find solutions after a crisis, it is important to realize that complex situations are impossible to fully understand or control. Instead, managers and co-workers need to accept and embrace that the organization's reality is ambiguous, with many different interpretations. This is the phase in which the organization has the opportunity to learn, and it is therefore important that managers continuously emphasize that people learn through mistakes and that we all make mistakes all the time. This will hopefully lead to a cultural change and contribute to deviation and weak signal reporting making its way to managers and that they, in turn, become listeners to their co-workers. vw did not listen to its co-workers, which had devastating effects on one of the world's largest car companies.

- *Try to identify blind spots:* One way of developing your understanding of what happened is by, together with your co-workers, identifying blind spots, that is, areas that you did not consider to be important but that played a large role in the development of the crisis. It is also important to ask why you didn't see these areas.

- *Develop internal communication:* If communication before and during the crisis was not satisfactory, it is important to, in the post-crisis phase, learn from it and try to develop internal communication for the future. Initially, it is necessary to map out weaknesses and to listen to the co-workers' needs and wishes regarding internal communication. After that, the communicators need to think about how the communication system will work in the future and what different forms of support and training are needed to improve internal communication. Support efforts should not only be directed toward managers but also toward the other co-workers, who need support in how to communicate and respond to, for example, irritated or angry customers. As co-workers are the most important ambassadors for the organization, it is also important that they have the support necessary to do their job well.

Chapter 8

A note on methodology

CASE STUDIES ARE a research strategy defined by a number of characteristics (Heide & Simonsson, 2014b). One characteristic is the study of a few units, such as an organization. Researchers who work with case studies are primarily interested in detail and in the particular rather than in the general. Instead of trying to find generalizations throughout many organizations, researchers choose to study one organization that is especially interesting from a certain angle. Researchers doing case studies try to get close to what is being studied and often combine interviews and observations to get rich empirical material. The goal is to study natural and concrete situations. Finally, many case studies contain analyses of several different levels within an organization in order to get as wide a picture as possible of what is being studied (see Eisenhardt, 1989).

Our case study was carried out over three years, with differing degrees of intensity. We used a number of different methods in order to get the richest and most nuanced material possible. The majority of our empirical material was gathered through interviews (both individual and in groups), but we also conducted observations and analyses of different types of documents. In total, we interviewed 39 people at the university hospital (33 individuals and two group interviews with three people in each group). Of these, 16 people were in charge of parts of the formal crisis management and crisis organization, 8 were communicators, and 15 people were working clinically at the emergency room in Malmö. We also observed a comprehensive crisis exercise and a number of meetings held in order to avoid and manage emerging problems regarding personnel and available beds during a holiday period. In addition to interviews and observations, we had access to a large number of internal documents such as crisis plans, crisis communication plans and other strategic documents. During the 3 years we studied the organization, we have also taken in a number of articles about the hospital published in *Sydsvenskan* – not because we conducted a content analysis of these articles, but because we wanted to increase our own understanding of the organization's external media image. During certain periods articles were published daily, and during other periods we found articles every week.

As the university hospital is a very large organization, we were unable to cover all clinics and departments. Instead, we chose to conduct different substudies that focused on different aspects of the organization as well as different departments and actors within the organization. We conducted four substudies:

1   The formal crisis preparedness and crisis management at the hospital
2   Professional communicators and communications work
3   Error management – an example of how a crisis can be avoided
4   The "expected" crisis – care capacity during the summer holidays

Initially, we focused on formal crisis organization and crisis management and how it can be understood from an internal communications perspective. In this case, the organization, as a whole, was our unit of analysis. We interviewed people who play a key role within formal crisis organization, such as members of the steering committee for crises and disasters, crisis coordinators, quality coordinators and chief surgeons. This study also included an observation of a major crisis exercise.

The second substudy placed the professional communicators and their role in internal communication in focus. Here, our unit of analysis was more a professional group than the organization as a whole. We interviewed both central communicators and those who were located in different divisions. We also asked managers questions about their view on the communicators' role and work.

In the third substudy, we aimed our focus on the attention given to error management in the emergency room. During the first substudy we found that the error reporting system could be seen as a part of the crisis management system, though it was not a formal part of that system. However, the interviews in this substudy demonstrated that error reporting is definitely a part of crisis management. Through reporting, early crisis signals and deviations can be caught by the staff. The emergency room is also particularly interesting here, as this department represents a kind of hub in the organization's crisis management system. We conducted individual interviews with managers and doctors, as well as group interviews with other healthcare professionals, in relation to this substudy.

The fourth substudy gave us the chance to study an "expected" crisis, that is to say, how being short-staffed and having too few beds during the summer holidays should be managed. This cannot be said to be a large, unexpected crisis, but at the same time the limited care capacity constitutes a recurring problem that often triggered the first emergency level. We observed several different meetings, such as meetings with operations managers before the summer as well as regular meetings during the summer wherein selected managers met to solve urgent problems. We supplemented these observations with interviews.

Researchers are rarely given the opportunity to study crises when they are actually in progress but normally are only able to study in retrospect. This is problematic, as stories of what happened tend to change, and there is a human tendency to forget or exaggerate the events. Simply put, it can be difficult to really understand what has happened. On the other hand, it may be difficult to study a crisis when it occurs as the people involved have not yet had distance or perspective on the events. The lack of beds and staff in the summer never developed into a "real" crisis, but it gave us insight into how communication and leadership work in a turbulent and strained situation. At the same time, the situation was not so chaotic that it was difficult to gain access to and understand what was happening.

We have used different interview guides in our substudies. The guides are made up of a number of questions, divided into four or five themes. The advantage of qualitative interviews is that the questions, follow-up questions and language can be adapted to the situation and the person being interviewed. We have also taken advantage of the opportunity to ask new questions and follow-up questions depending on what comes up during the interview. As a result, we have been able to "dig deeper" in some areas where the interviewee has particularly deep knowledge or experience. Furthermore, we have included earlier results into the next interviews and phase, thereby being able to deepen our own knowledge step by step. In other words, our study is process-oriented. We also depart from the assumption that processes in organizations are more important than stable situations. Organizations are never static or physical objects that are easy to study. Karl E. Weick (e.g., 1995, 2009; Weick et al., 2005) is the researcher who has led the way for a process-oriented perspective on organizational studies.

References

Alexander, D. E. (2013). Resilience and disaster risk reduction: An etymological journey. *Natural Hazards & Earth System Sciences, 13*(11), 2707–2716.

Altheide, D. L., & Snow, R. P. (1979). *Media logic.* Beverly Hills, CA: Sage.

Alvesson, M. (2004). *Knowledge work and knowledge-intensive firms.* Oxford: Oxford University Press.

Alvesson, M. (2013). *Organisation och ledning. Ett något skeptiskt perspektiv.* Lund: Studentlitteratur.

Alvesson, M., & Kärreman, D. (2001). Odd couple: Making sense of the curious concept of knowledge management. *Journal of Management Studies, 38*(7), 995–1018.

Alvesson, M., & Spicer, A. (2010). Theories of leadership. In M. Alvesson & A. Spicer (Eds.), *Metaphors we lead by: Understanding leadership in the real world* (pp. 8–30). New York, NY: Routledge.

Alvesson, M., & Spicer, A. (2011). *Metaphors we lead by: Understanding leadership in the real world.* New York, NY: Routledge.

Alvesson, M., & Spicer, A. (2012). A stupidity-based theory of organizations. *Journal of Management Studies, 49*(7), 1194–1220.

Alvesson, M., & Sveningsson, S. (2015). *Changing organizational culture: Cultural change work in progress* (2nd ed.). London: Routledge.

Ancona, D., Malone, T. W., Orlikowski, W. J., & Senge, P. M. (2007). In praise of the incomplete [leadership]. *Harvard Business Review, 85*(2), 92–100.

Andersen, P. A., & Spitzberg, B. H. (2009). Myths and maxims of risk and crisis communication. In R. L. Heath & H. D. O'Hair (Eds.), *Handbook of risk and crisis communication* (pp. 205–226). New York, NY: Routledge.

Ansell, C., Boin, A., & Keller, A. (2010). Managing transboundary crises: Identifying the building blocks of an effective response system. *Journal of Contingencies & Crisis Management, 18*(4), 195–207.

Argyris, C. (1977). Double loop learning in organizations. *Harvard Business Review, 55*(5), 115–125.

Argyris, C. (1994). Good communication that blocks learning. *Harvard Business Review, 72*(3), 74–85.

Argyris, C., & Schön, D. A. (1978). *Organizational learning*. Reading, MA: Addison-Wesley.

Ashcraft, K. L., & Trethewey, A. (2004). Developing tension: An agenda for applied research on the organization of irrationality. *Journal of Applied Communication Research, 32*(2), 171–181.

Balogun, J., Best, K., & Lê, J. (2015). Selling the object of strategy: How frontline workers realize strategy through their daily work. *Organization Studies, 36*(10), 1285–1313.

Balogun, J., & Johnson, G. (2004). Organizational restructuring and middle manager sensemaking. *Academy of Management Journal, 47*(4), 523–549.

Baran, B. E., & Scott, C. W. (2010). Organizing ambiguity: A grounded theory of leadership and sensemaking within dangerous contexts. *Military Psychology, 22*, 42–69.

Barthol, R. P., & Ku, N. D. (1959). Regression under stress to first learned behavior. *Journal of Abnormal Psychology, 59*(1), 134–136.

Barton, M. A., Sutcliffe, K. M., Vogus, T. J., & DeWitt, T. (2015). Performing under uncertainty: Contextualized engagement in wildland firefighting. *Journal of Contingencies and Crisis Management, 23*(2), 74–83.

Bateson, G. (1972). *Steps to an ecology of mind*. Chicago, IL: The University of Chicago Press.

Bechler, C. (2004). Reframing the organizational exigency: Taking a new approach in crisis research. In D. P. Millar & R. L. Heath (Eds.), *Responding to crisis: A rhetorical approach to crisis communication* (pp. 63–74). London: Lawrence Erlbaum Associates.

Beck, U. (1992). *Risk society: Towards a new modernity*. London: Sage.

Benoit, W. L. (1997). Image repair discourse and crisis communication. *Public Relations Review, 23*(2), 177–186.

Berger, P. L., & Luckmann, T. (1966). *The social construction of reality: A treatise in the sociology of knowledge*. New York, NY: Doubleday.

Berlin, J., & Kastberg, G. (2011). *Styrning av hälso- och sjukvård*. Malmö: Liber.

Bisel, R. S., & Arterburn, E. N. (2012). Making sense of organizational members' silence: A sensemaking-resource model. *Communication Research Reports, 29*(3), 217–226.

Boholm, Å., & Corvellec, H. (2011). A relational theory of risk. *Journal of Risk Research, 14*(2), 175–190.

Boin, A., Kuipers, S., & Overdijk, W. (2013). Leadership in times of crisis: A framework for assessment. *International Review of Public Administration, 18*(1), 79–91.

Boin, A., McConnell, A., & 't Hart, P. (2008). *Governing after crisis: The politics of investigation, accountability and learning*. Cambridge: Cambridge University Press.

Boin, A., 't Hart, P., Stern, E. K., & Sundelius, B. (2005). *The politics of crisis management: Public leadership under pressure*. Cambridge: Cambridge University Press.

Boje, D. M. (1994). Organizational storytelling: The struggles of pre-modern, modern and postmodern organizational learning discourses. *Management Learning, 25*(3), 433–461.

Bozeman, B. (2011). Toward a theory of organizational implosion. *American Review of Public Administration, 41*(2), 119–140.

Breit, E. (2014). Remedy through paradox? Constructions of internal legitimacy in a publicly discredited organization. *Management Communication Quarterly, 28*(4), 585–608.

Brown, A. D., & Starkey, K. (2000). Organizational identity and learning: A psychodynamic perspective. *The Academy of Management Review, 25*(1), 102–120.

Brown, J. S., & Duguid, P. (1991). Organizational learning and communities-of-practice: Toward a unified view of working, learning, and innovation. *Organization Science, 2*(1), 40–57.

Brown, S. L., & Eisenhardt, K. M. (1997). The art of continuous change: Linking complexity theory and time-paced evolution in relentlessly shifting organizations. *Administrative Science Quarterly, 42*(1), 1–34.

Bruner, J. S. (1983). *In search of mind: Essays in autobiography.* New York, NY: Harper & Row.

Bruner, J. S. (1990). *Acts of meaning.* Cambridge, MA: Harvard University Press.

Brunsson, N. (1982). The irrationality of action and action rationality: Decisions, ideologies and organizational actions. *The Journal of Management Studies, 19*(1), 29–45.

Burris, E. R. (2012). The risks and rewards of speaking up: Managerial responses to employee voice. *Academy of Management Journal, 55*(4), 851–875.

Carey, J. (2009). *Communication as culture: Essays on media and society.* New York, NY: Routledge.

Carroll, J. S. (2015). Making sense of ambiguity through dialogue and collaborative action. *Journal of Contingencies and Crisis Management, 23*(2), 59–65.

Cheney, G., Christensen, L. T., Zorn, T. E., & Ganesh, S. (Eds.). (2011). *Organizational communication in an age of globalization: Issues, reflections, practices* (2nd ed.). Long Grove, IL: Waveland Press.

Christianson, M. K., Farkas, M. T., Sutcliffe, K. M., & Weick, K. E. (2009). Learning through rare events: Significant interruptions at the Baltimore & Ohio Railroad Museum. *Organization Science, 20*(5), 846–860.

Christianson, M. K., Sutcliffe, K. M., Miller, M. A., & Iwashyna, T. J. (2011). Becoming a high reliability organization. *Critical Care, 15*(6), 1–5.

Clarke, L. (1999). *Mission improbable: Using fantasy documents to tame disaster.* Chicago, IL: The University of Chicago Press.

Collinson, D. (2006). Rethinking followership: A post-structuralist analysis of follower identities. *The Leadership Quarterly, 17*, 179–189.

Coombs, W. T. (2006). Crisis management: A communicative approach. In C. H. Botan & V. Hazleton (Eds.), *Public relations theory II* (pp. 171–197). Mahwah, NJ: Lawrence Erlbaum Associates.

Coombs, W. T. (2007). Attribution theory as a guide for post-crisis communication research. *Public Relations Review, 33*, 135–139.

Coombs, W. T. (2010). Crisis communication and its allied fields. In W. T. Coombs & S. J. Holladay (Eds.), *The handbook of crisis communication* (pp. 54–64). Malden, MA: Blackwell Publishing.

Coombs, W. T. (2019). *Ongoing crisis communication: Planning, managing, and responding.* Thousand Oaks, CA: Sage.

Coombs, W. T., & Holladay, S. H. (Eds.). (2010). *The handbook of crisis communication*. Malden, MA: Blackwell Publishing.

Cunha, M. P. E., Clegg, S., Rego, A. N., & Neves, P. (2014). Organizational improvisation: From the constraint of strict tempo to the power of the avant-garde. *Creativity and Innovation Management, 23*(4), 359–373.

Cunha, M. P. E., Rego, A., Clegg, S., & Lindsay, G. (2015). The dialectics of serendipity. *European Management Journal, 33*(1), 9–18.

Cyert, R. M., & March, J. G. (1963). *A behavioral theory of the firm.* Englewood Cliffs, NJ: Prentice Hall.

Day, G., & Schoemaker, P. (2008). Are you a vigilant leader? *MIT Sloan Management Review, Spring,* 43–51.

de Bussy, N. M., & Wolf, K. (2008). The state of Australian public relations: Professionalisation and paradox. *Public Relations Review, 35*(4), 376–381.

Deetz, S. A. (1992). *Democracy in an age of corporate colonization: Development in communication and the politics of everyday life.* Albany: State University of New York Press.

Deetz, S. A., Tracey, S., & Simpson, J. (2000). *Leading organizations through transitions: Communication and cultural change.* Thousand Oaks, CA: Sage.

Deverell, E. (2009). Crises as learning triggers: Exploring a conceptual framework of crisis-induced learning. *Journal of Contingencies & Crisis Management, 17*(3), 179–188.

Deverell, E. (2010). Flexibility and rigidity in crisis management and learning at Swedish public organizations. *Public Management Review, 12*(5), 679–700.

Douglas, M., & Wildavsky, A. (1983). *Risk and culture.* Berkley, CA: University of California Press.

Drennan, L. T., McConnell, A., & Stark, A. (2014). *Risk and crisis management in the public sector.* New York, NY: Routledge.

Edmondson, A. C. (2003). Speaking up in the operating room: How team leaders promote learning in interdisciplinary action teams. *Journal of Management Studies, 40*(6), 1419–1452.

Eisenhardt, K. M. (1989). Building theories from case study research. *Academy of Management Review, 14*(4), 532–550.

Eriksson, M. (2009). *Nätens kriskommunikation.* Lund: Studentlitteratur.

Fairhurst, G. T. (2001). Dualisms in leadership research. In F. M. Jablin & L. L. Putnam (Eds.), *The new handbook of organizational communication: Advances in theory, research and methods* (pp. 379–439). Thousand Oaks, CA: Sage.

Fairhurst, G. T., & Sarr, R. A. (1996). *The art of framing: Managing the language of leadership.* San Francisco, CA: Jossey-Bass Publishers.

Falkheimer, J., & Heide, M. (2010). Crisis communicators in change: From plans to improvisations. In W. T. Coombs & S. Holladay (Eds.), *Handbook of crisis communication* (pp. 511–526). Malden, MA: Wiley-Blackwell.

Falkheimer, J., & Heide, M. (2015). Trust and brand recovery campaigns in crisis: Findus Nordic and the horsemeat scandal. *International Journal of Strategic Communication, 9*(2), 134–147.

Falkheimer, J., Heide, M., & Larsson, L. (2009). *Kriskommunikation.* Malmö: Liber.

Fearn-Banks, K. (2016). *Crisis communications: A casebook approach* (5th ed.). New York, NY: Routledge.

Festinger, L. (1983). *The human legacy*. New York, NY: Columbia University Press.

Fink, S. (1986). *Crisis management: Planning for the inevitable*. New York, NY: American Management Association.

Frandsen, F., & Johansen, W. (2011). The study of internal crisis communication: Towards an integrative framework. *Corporate Communications: An International Journal, 16*(4), 347–361.

Frandsen, F., & Johansen, W. (2017). *Organizational crisis communication*. London: Sage.

Galpin, S., & Sims, D. (1999). Narratives and identity in flexible working and teleworking organisations. In P. J. Jackson (Eds.), *Virtual working: Social and organizational dynamics* (pp. 76–94). London: Routledge.

Gilpin, D. R., & Murphy, P. J. (2008). *Crisis communication in a complex world*. Oxford: Oxford University Press.

Gilpin, D. R., & Murphy, P. J. (2010). Complexity and crises: A new paradigm. In W. T. Coombs & S. J. Holladay (Eds.), *The handbook of crisis communication* (pp. 683–690). Malden, MA: Wiley-Blackwell.

Goodman, P. S., Ramanujam, R., Carroll, J. S., Edmondson, A. C., Hofmann, D. A., & Sutcliffe, K. M. (2011). Organizational errors: Directions for future research. *Research in Organizational Behavior, 31*(1), 151–176.

Grint, K. (2005). Problems, problems, problems: The social construction of "leadership". *Human Relations, 58*(11), 1467–1494.

Grunig, J. E. (1975). A multi-systems theory of organizational communication. *Communication Research, 2*(2), 99–133.

Grunig, J. E., Grunig, L. A., & Dozier, D. M. (2006). The excellence theory. In C. H. Botan & V. Hazleton (Eds.), *Public relations theory II* (pp. 21–62). Mahwah, NJ: Lawrence Erlbaum Associates.

Guldenmund, F. W. (2000). The nature of safety culture: A review of theory and research. *Safety Science, 34*, 215–257.

Habermas, J. (1995). *Kommunikativt handlande: Texter om språk, rationalitet och samhälle* (2 uppl.). Göteborg: Daidalos.

Hassan, F. (2011). The frontline advantage. *Harvard Business Review, 89*(5), 106–114.

Hayes, A. F., Glynn, C. J., & Shanahan, J. (2005). Willingness to self-censor: A construct and measurement tool for public opinion research. *International Journal of Public Opinion Research, 17*(3), 298–323.

Heath, R. L. (2010). Introduction. In T. W. Coombs & S. J. Holladay (Eds.), *The handbook of crisis communication* (pp. 1–13). Malden, MA: Wiley-Blackwell.

Heath, R. L., & Millar, D. P. (2004). A rhetorical approach to crisis communication: Management, communication processes, and strategic responses. In D. P. Millar & R. L. Heath (Eds.), *Responding to crisis: A rhetorical approach to crisis communication* (pp. 1–17). Mahwah, NJ: Lawrence Erlbaum Associates.

Heath, R. L., & O'Hair, D. (2009). *Handbook of risk and crisis communication*. New York, NY: Routledge.

Hedberg, B. (1981). How organizations learn and unlearn. In P. C. Nystrom & W. H. Starbuck (Eds.), *Handbook of organizational design, Vol. 1: Adapting organizations to their environments* (pp. 3–26). New York, NY: Oxford University Press.

Heide, M. (2002). *Intranät: En ny arena för kommunikation och lärande*. Lund: Lunds universitet, Sociologiska institutionen.

Heide, M., Johansson, C., & Simonsson, C. (2012). *Kommunikation & organisation.* Malmö: Liber.

Heide, M., & Simonsson, C. (2011). Putting co-workers in the limelight: New challenges for communication professionals. *International Journal of Strategic Communication, 5*(4), 201–220.

Heide, M., & Simonsson, C. (2013). *Errors in organizations: Opportunities for crisis management,* The Conference on Corporate Communication 2013, June 4–7, Baruch College/CUNY, New York, NY, USA.

Heide, M., & Simonsson, C. (2014a). Developing internal crisis communication: New roles and practices of communication professionals. *Corporate Communications: An International Journal, 19*(2), 128–146.

Heide, M., & Simonsson, C. (2014b). Kvalitet och kunskap i fallstudier. In J. Eksell & Å. Thelander (Eds.), *Kvalitativa metoder i strategisk kommunikation* (pp. 215–232). Lund: Studentlitteratur.

Heide, M., & Simonsson, C. (2015). Struggling with internal crisis communication: A balancing act between paradoxical tensions. *Public Relations Inquiry, 4*(2), 223–255.

Heide, M., & Simonsson, C. (forthcoming). Internal crisis communication: On current and future research. In F. Frandsen & W. Johansen (Eds.), *Handbooks of communication science* (Vol. 23). Berlin: De Gruyter Mouton.

Hennestad, B. D. (1990). The symbolic impact of double bind and leadership: Double bind and the dynamics of organizational culture. *Journal of Management Studies, 27*(3), 265–280.

Hermann, C. F. (1963). Some consequences of crisis which limit the viability of organizations. *Administrative Science Quarterly, 8*(1), 61–82.

Hernes, T., & Irgens, E. J. (2012). Keeping things mindfully on track: Organizational learning under continuity. *Management Learning, 44*(3), 253–266.

Hofman, D. A., & Frese, M. (2011). Errors, error taxonomies, error prevention, and error management: Laying the groundwork for discussing errors in organizations. In D. A. Hofman & M. Frese (Eds.), *Errors in organizations* (pp. 1–43). New York, NY: Routledge.

Holt, R., & Cornelissen, J. (2014). Sensemaking revisited. *Management Learning, 45*(5), 525–539.

Holtzhausen, D. R. (2012). *Public relations as activism: Postmodern approaches to theory and practice.* New York, NY: Routledge.

Huber, G. P. (1991). Organizational learning: The contributing processes and the literatures. *Organization Science, 2*(1), 88–115.

Huber, G. P. (2004). *The necessary nature of future firms.* Thousand Oaks, CA: Sage.

Hunter, S. T., Tate, B. W., Dzieweczynski, J. L., & Bedell-Avers, K. E. (2011). Leaders make mistakes: A multilevel consideration of why. *The Leadership Quarterly, 22*(2), 239–258.

Jackson, B., & Parry, K. W. (2011). *A very short fairly interesting and reasonably cheap book about studying leadership.* London: Sage.

James, E. H., & Wooten, L. P. (2005). Leadership as (un) usual: How to display competence in times of crisis. *Organizational Dynamics, 32*(2), 141–152.

James, E. H., Wooten, P. L., & Dushek, K. (2011). Crisis management: Informing a new leadership research agenda. *The Academy of Management Annals, 5*(11), 455–493.

Janis, I. L. (1982). *Groupthink: Psychological studies of policy decisions and fiascoes* (2nd ed.). Boston, MA: Houghton Mifflin.

Johansen, W., Aggerholm, H. K., & Frandsen, F. (2012). Entering new territory: A study of internal crisis management and crisis communication in organizations. *Public Relations Review, 38*(2), 270–279.

Johansen, W., & Frandsen, F. (2007). *Krisekommunikation: Når virksomhedens image og omdømme er truet.* Köpenhamn: Samfundslitteratur.

Kåver, A. (2004). *Att leva ett liv, inte vinna ett krig: Om acceptans.* Stockholm: Natur Kultur.

Kent, M. L. (2010). What is a public relations "crisis"? Refocusing crisis research. In T. W. Coombs & S. J. Holladay (Eds.), *The handbook of crisis communication* (pp. 705–712). Malden, MA: Wiley-Blackwell.

Kersten, A. (2005). Crisis as usual: Organizational dysfunction and public relations. *Public Relations Review, 31*(4), 544–549.

Kim, Y. M., & Newby-Bennett, D. (2012). The role of leadership in learning culture and patient safety. *International Journal of Organization Theory and Behavior, 15*(2), 151–175.

Knudsen, G. H., & Lemmergaard, J. (2014). Strategic serendipity: How one organization planned for and took advantage of unexpected communicative opportunities. *Culture and Organization, 20*(5), 392–409.

Kohn, L. T., Corrigan, J. M., & Donaldson, M. S. (2000). *To err is human: Building a safer health system.* Washington, DC: National Academy Press.

Kopaneva, I. M. (2015, digital publication). Left in the dust: Employee constructions of mission and vision ownership. *International Journal of Business Communication.* Retrieved October 29, 2015, from http://job.sagepub.com/content/early/2015/09/15/2329488415604457.abstract

Korn, C., & Einwiller, S. (2013). Media coverage about organisations in critical situations: Analysing the impact on employees. *Corporate Communications: An International Journal, 18*(4), 451–468.

Kukule, L. (2014). *Internal communication crisis: Impact on organization's performance.* Saarbrücken: Lambert Academic Publishing.

Lagadec, P. (1993). *Preventing chaos in a crisis: Strategies for prevention, control and damage limitation.* London: McGraw-Hill.

La Porte, T. R. (1996). High reliability organizations: Unlikely, demanding and at risk. *Journal of Contingencies & Crisis Management, 4*(2), 60–71.

La Porte, T. R., & Consolini, P. M. (1991). Working in practice but not in theory: Theoretical challenges of "high-reliability organizations". *Journal of Public Administration Research and Theory, 1*(1), 19–48.

Lerbringer, O. (1997). *The crisis manager: Facing risk and responsibility.* Mahwah, NJ: Lawrence Erlbaum Associates.

Lerbringer, O. (2012). *Crisis manager: Facing disasters, conflicts, and failures.* New York, NY: Routledge.

Levay, C. (2009). Karismatiskt ledarskap. In L. Strannegård & S. Jönsson (Eds.), *Ledarskapsboken* (pp. 316–331). Malmö: Liber.

Lewis, M. W. (2000). Exploring paradox: Toward a more comprehensive guide. *Academy of Management Review, 25*(4), 760–776.

Maitlis, S., & Sonenshein, S. (2010). Sensemaking in crisis and change: Inspiration and insights from Weick (1988). *Journal of Management Studies, 47*(3), 551–580.

Marra, F. J. (1998). Crisis communication plans: Poor predictors of excellent crisis public relations. *Public Relations Review, 24*(4), 461–474.

Marra, F. J. (2004). Excellent crisis communication: Beyond crisis plans. In D. P. Millar & R. L. Heath (Eds.), *Responding to crisis: A rhetorical approach to crisis communication* (pp. 311–326). Mahwah, NJ: Lawrence Erlbaum Associates.

Mathisen Dietrichson, L. (2013). *Den hotande krisen: Om kommunikation kring hot och våld på en akutmottagning* (examensarbete för mastersexamen). Lund: Lunds universitet, Institutionen för strategisk kommunikation.

Mazzei, A. (2010). Promoting active communication behaviours through internal communication. *Corporate Communications: An International Journal, 15*(3), 221–234.

Mazzei, A., Kim, J.-N., & Dell'Oro, C. (2012). Strategic value of employee relationships and communicative actions: Overcoming corporate crisis with quality internal communication. *International Journal of Strategic Communication, 6*(1), 31–44.

Mazzei, A., & Ravazzani, S. (2011). Manager-employee communication during a crisis: The missing link. *Corporate Communications: An International Journal, 16*(3), 243–254.

Mazzei, A., & Ravazzani, S. (2015). Internal crisis communication strategies to protect trust relationships: A study of Italian companies. *International Journal of Business Communication, 52*(3), 319–337.

Meacham, J. A. (1983). Wisdom and the context of knowledge. In D. Kuhn & J. A. Meacham (Eds.), *On the development of developmental psychology, vol. 8: Contributions in human development* (pp. 111–134). Basel: Karger.

Megginson, D. (1996). Planned and emergent learning: Consequences for development. *Management Learning, 27*(4), 411–428.

Mercer, L., & Kapcio, P. (2006). Internal communications for the avian flu: Anticipating effects on lives and livelihoods. *Public Relations Tactics, 13*(7), 20–22.

Meyers, G. C. (1987). *When it hits the fan: Managing the nine crises of business.* London: Unwin Hyman.

Millar, D. P. (2004). Exposing the errors: An examination of the nature of organizational crises. In D. P. Millar & R. L. Heath (Eds.), *Responding to crisis: A rhetorical approach to crisis communication* (pp. 19–31). Mahwah, NJ: Lawrence Erlbaum Associates.

Mintzberg, H. (2009). *Structure in fives: Designing effective organizations* (2nd ed.). Harlow, Essex: Pearson Education.

Mitroff, I. I. (1994). Crisis management and environmentalism: A natural fit. *California Management Review, 36*(2), 101–114.

Mitroff, I. I. (2001). Crisis leadership. *Executive Excellence, 18*(8), 19.

Mitroff, I. I. (2004). *Crisis leadership: Planning for the unthinkable.* Hoboken, NJ: John Wiley & Sons.

Muffet-Willett, S. L., & Kruse, S. D. (2009). Crisis leadership: Past research and future directions. *Journal of Business Continuity & Emergency Planning, 3*(3), 248–258.

Neuman-Neulle, E. (1993). *The spiral of silence*. London: The University of Chicago Press.

Nicolini, D., & Meznar, M. B. (1995). The social construction of organizational learning: Conceptual and practical issues in the field. *Human Relations, 48*(7), 727–746.

Olaniran, B. A. (2007). The role of perception in crisis management: A tale of two hurricanes. *Multicultural Education, 15*(2), 13–16.

Orr, J. E. (1996). *Talking about machines: An ethnography of a modern job*. Ithaca, NY: Cornell University Press.

Palenchar, M. (2009). Historical trends of risk and crisis communication. In R. L. Heath & D. H. O'Hair (Eds.), *Handbook of risk and crisis communication* (pp. 31–52). New York, NY: Routledge.

Palm, L., & Falkheimer, J. (2005). *Förtroendekriser – kommunikationsstrategier före, under och efter* (KBM:s temaserie). Stockholm: KBM.

Parry, K. W., & Bryman, A. (2006). Leadership in organizations. In S. R. Clegg, C. Hardy, T. B. Lawrence, & W. R. Nord (Eds.), *The Sage handbook of organization studies* (pp. 547–468). London: Sage.

Pauchant, T. C., & Mitroff, I. I. (1992). *Transforming the crisis-prone organization: Preventing individual, organizational, and environmental tragedies*. San Francisco, CA: Jossey-Bass Publishers.

Penrose, J. M. (2000). The role of perception in crisis planning. *Public Relations Review, 26*(2), 155–177.

Perrow, C. (1977). The bureaucratic paradox: The efficient organization centralizes in order to decentralize. *Organizational Dynamics, 5*(4), 3–14.

Perrow, C. (1984). *Normal accidents: Living with high-risk technologies*. New York, NY: Basic Books.

Perrow, C. (1994). The limits of safety: The enhancements of a theory of accidents. *Journal of Contingencies & Crisis Management, 2*(4), 212–221.

Raelin, J. A. (2015). Rethinking leadership. *MIT Sloan Management Review, 56*(4), 96–97.

Ravazzani, S. (2016). Exploring internal crisis communication in multicultural environments. *Corporate Communications: An International Journal, 21*(1), 73–88.

Reason, J. (1990). *Human error*. Cambridge: Cambridge University Press.

Reason, J. (2000). Human error: Models and management. *British Medical Journal, 320*(7237), 768–770.

Renn, O. (1992). Concepts of risk: A classification. In S. Krimsky & D. Golding (Eds.), *Social theories of risk* (pp. 53–79). Westport, CT: Praeger.

Roberts, K. H. (1990). Some characteristics of one type of high reliability organization. *Organization Science, 1*(2), 160–176.

Roberts, K. H., & O'Reilly, R. (1974). Failures in upward communication in organizations: Three possible culprits. *The Academy of Management Journal, 17*(2), 205–215.

Rosenthal, U., Boin, R. A., & Comfort, L. K. (2001). *Managing crises: Threats, dilemmas, opportunities*. Springfield, IL: Charles C Thomas.

Roux-Dufort, C. (2007). Is crisis management (only) a management of exceptions? *Journal of Contingencies and Crisis Management, 15*(2), 105–114.

Ruchlin, H. S., Dubbs, N. L., & Callahan, M. A. (2004). The role of leadership in instilling a culture of safety: Lessons from the literature. *Journal of Healthcare Management, 49*(1), 47–59.

Sagan, S. D. (1993). *The limits of safety: Organizations, accidents and nuclear weapons.* Princeton, NJ: Princeton University Press.

Seeger, M. W., Sellnow, T. L., & Ulmer, R. R. (2003). *Communication and organizational crisis.* Westport, CT: Praeger.

Sellnow, T. L., & Seeger, M. W. (2013). *Theorizing crisis communication.* Malden, MA: Wiley-Blackwell.

Senge, P. M. (1990). *The fifth discipline: The art & practice of the learning organization.* New York, NY: Currency Doubleday.

Shamir, B. (2007). From passive recipients to active co-producers: Followers' roles in the leadership process. In B. Shamir, R. Pillai, M. C. Bligh, & M. Uhl-Bien (Eds.), *Follower-centered perspectives on leadership: A tribute to the memory of James R. Meindl* (s. ix–xxxix). Greenwich, CT: Information Age Publishing.

Shojaie, S., Matin, H. Z., & Barani, G. (2011). Analyzing the infrastructures of organizational silence and ways to get rid of it. *Social and Behavioral Sciences, 30,* 1731–1735.

Sigrell, A. (2011). Att föreläsa är att lyssna. Om retorik som konsten att lyssna. In A. Skodvin, K. H. Fluym, G. Knudsen, & E. Simonsen (Eds.), *Forelesningens kunst* (pp. 29–51). Oslo: Litteraturhuset.

Simon, H. A. (1957). *Models of man, social and rational: Mathematical essays on rational human behavior in a social setting.* New York, NY: Wiley-Blackwell.

Simonet, D. (2008). The new public management theory and European healthcare reforms. *Canadian Public Administration, 51*(4), 617–635.

Simonsen, D. M. (2015). *Organisatorisk resiliens fra et kommunikativt perspektiv* (avhandling för doktorsexamen). Aarhus: Aarhus Universitet, Institut for Erhvervskommunikation.

Simonsson, C. (2011). Vem leder vem? Om kommunikationen mellan medarbetare och ledare. In J. Falkheimer & M. Heide (Eds.), *Strategisk kommunikation: Forskning och praktik* (pp. 235–253). Lund: Studentlitteratur.

Simonsson, C., & Heide, M. (2018). How focusing positively on errors can help organizations become more communicative: An alternative approach to crisis communication. *Journal of Communication Management, 22*(2), 179–196.

Sims, D. (1999). Organizational learning as the development of stories: Canons, apocrypha and pious myths. In M. Easterby-Smith, J. Burgoyne, & L. Araujo (Eds.), *Organizational learning and the learning organization: Developments in theory and practice* (pp. 44–58). London: Sage.

Sims, D. (2010). Looking for the key to leadership under the lamp post. *European Management Journal, 28,* 253–259.

Skivenes, M., & Trygstad Sissel, C. (2010). When whistle-blowing works: The norwegian case. *Human Relations, 63*(7), 1071–1097.

Smircich, L. (1983). Implications for management theory. In L. L. Putnam & M. E. Pacanowsky (Eds.), *Communication and organizations: An interpretive approach* (pp. 221–242). London: Sage.

150 References

Smircich, L., & Morgan, G. (1982). Leadership: The management of meaning. *The Journal of Applied Behavioral Science, 18*(3), 257–273.

Smith, D., & Elliott, D. (2007). Exploring the barriers to learning from crisis: Organizational learning and crisis. *Management Learning, 38*(5), 519–538.

Smith, W. K., & Lewis, M. W. (2011). Toward a theory of paradox: A dynamic equilibrium model of organizing. *Academy of Management Review, 36*(2), 381–403.

Sohn, Y. J., & Lariscy, R. W. (2014). Understanding reputational crisis: Definition, properties, and consequences. *Journal of Public Relations Research, 26*(1), 23–43.

Stock, G. N., McFadden, K. L., & Gowen, C. R., III. (2006). Organizational culture, critical success factors, and the reduction of hospital errors. *International Journal of Production Economics, 106*, 368–392.

Strandberg, J. M., & Vigsø, O. (2016). Internal crisis communication. *Corporate Communications: An International Journal, 21*(1), 89–102.

Sturges, D. L. (1994). Communicating through crisis: A strategy for organizational survival. *Management Communication Quarterly, 7*(3), 297–316.

Sutcliffe, K. M. (2001). Organizational environments and organizational information processing. In F. M. Jablin & L. L. Putnam (Eds.), *The new handbook of organizational communication: Advances in theory, research, and methods* (pp. 197–230). Thousand Oaks, CA: Sage.

Sutcliffe, K. M. (2011). High reliability organizations (HROs). *Best Practice & Research Clinical Anaesthesiology, 25*(2), 133–144.

Sutcliffe, K. M., & Vogus, T. J. (2003). Organizing for resilience. In K. Cameron, J. E. Dutton, & R. E. Quinn (Eds.), *Positive organizational scholarship* (pp. 94–110). San Francisco, CA: Berrett-Koehler.

Sveiby, K. E. (1990). *Kunskapsledning: 101 råd till ledare i kunskapsintensiva organisationer.* Stockholm: Affärsvärlden.

Sveningsson, S., & Alvesson, M. (2016). *Managerial lives: Leadership and identity in an imperfect world.* Cambridge: Cambridge University Press.

Svensson, L. G. (2002). *Professionella arbetsorganisationer: Arbetsvillkor och kompetensutveckling i universitets-och IT-sektorn* (Research Report at the Department of Sociology, Göteborg University no 127). Göteborg: Göteborgs universitet, Sociologiska institutionen. Tillgänglig. Retrieved from https://gupea.ub.gu.se/bitstream/2077/23155/1/gupea_2077_23155_1.pdf

Taylor, M. (2010). Towards a holistic organizational approach to understanding crisis. In W. T. Coombs & S. J. Holladay (Eds.), *The handbook of crisis communication* (pp. 698–704). Malden, MA: Wiley-Blackwell.

't Hart, P., Heyse, L., & Boin, A. (2001). Guest editorial introduction. New trends in crisis management practice and crisis management research: Setting the agenda. *Journal of Contingencies and Crisis Management, 9*(4), 181–188.

Thornblad, H. (2012). *De fick årets visslare och friska sjukvårdspriset.* Retrieved February 14, 2013, from www.sjukhuslakaren.se/2012/09/12/de-fick-arets-visslare-och-friska-sjukvardspriset/

Tourish, D. (2005). Critical upward communication: Ten commandments for improving strategy and decision making. *Long Range Planning, 38*(5), 485–503.

Tourish, D., & Hargie, O. (2004). Motivating critical upward communication: A key challenge for management decision making. In D. Tourish & O. Hargie (Eds.), *Key issues in organizational communication* (pp. 188–204). London: Routledge.

Tourish, D., & Robson, P. (2003). Critical upward feedback in organisations: Processes, problems and implications for communication management. *Journal of Communication Management, 8*(2), 150–168.

Tourish, D., & Robson, P. (2006). Sensemaking and the distortion of critical upward communication in organizations. *Journal of Management Studies, 43*(4), 711–730.

Tracey, K. (2002). *Everyday talk: Building and reflecting identities.* New York, NY: Guilford Press.

Turner, B. A. (1976). The organizational and interorganizational development of disasters. *Administrative Science Quarterly, 21*, 378–397.

Turner, B. A. (1994). Causes of disaster: Sloppy management. *British Journal of Management, 5*(3), 215–219.

Tyler, L. (2005). Towards a postmodern understanding of crisis communication. *Public Relations Review, 31*(4), 566–571.

Ulmer, R. R. (2012). Increasing the impact of thought leadership in crisis communication. *Management Communication Quarterly, 26*(4), 527–547.

Ulmer, R. R., Sellnow, T. L., & Seeger, M. W. (2007). *Effective crisis communication: Moving from crisis to opportunity.* Thousand Oaks, CA: Sage.

Ulmer, R. R., Sellnow, T. L., & Seeger, M. W. (2011). *Effective crisis communication: Moving from crisis to opportunity* (2nd ed.). London: Sage.

van Dyck, C., Frese, M., Baer, M., & Sonnentag, S. (2005). Organizational error management culture and its impact on performance: A two-study replication. *Journal of Applied Psychology, 90*(6), 1228–1240.

van Laere, J. (2013). Wandering through crisis and everyday organizing: Revealing the subjective nature of interpretive, temporal and organizational boundaries. *Journal of Contingencies and Crisis Management, 21*(1), 17–25.

Vigsø, O. (2015). *Krisekommunikation.* Frederiksberg: Samfundslitteratur.

Wan, H. H., & Pfau, M. (2004). The relative effectiveness of inoculation, bolstering, and combined approaches in crisis communication. *Journal of Public Relations Research, 16*(3), 301–328.

Ware, B. L., & Linkugel, W. A. (1973). They spoke in defense of themselves: On the generic criticism of apologia. *Quarterly Journal of Speech, 59*(3), 273–283.

Watzlawick, P., Beavin, J. H., & Jackson, D. P. (1967). *Pragamatics of human communication: A study of interactional patterns, pathologies, and paradoxes.* New York, NY: Norton.

Weick, K. E. (1987). Organizational culture as a source of high reliability. *California Management Review, 29*(2), 112–127.

Weick, K. E. (1988). Enacted sensemaking in crisis situations. *Journal of Management Studies, 25*, 305–317.

Weick, K. E. (1990). The vulnerable system: An analysis of the Tenerife air disaster. *Journal of Management, 16*(3), 571–593.

Weick, K. E. (1993). The collapse of sensemaking in organizations: The Mann Gulch disaster. *Administrative Science Quarterly, 38*(4), 628–652.

Weick, K. E. (1995). *Sensemaking in organizations.* Thousand Oaks, CA: Sage.

Weick, K. E. (1996). Drop your tools: An allegory for organizational studies. *Administrative Science Quarterly, 41*(2), 301–313.

Weick, K. E. (1998). Improvisation as a mindset for organizational analysis. *Organization Science: A Journal of the Institute of Management Sciences, 9*(5), 543–556.

Weick, K. E. (2009). *Making sense of the organization: The impermanent organization.* Chichester: John Wiley & Sons.

Weick, K. E. (2010). Reflections on enacted sensemaking in the Bhopal disaster. *Journal of Management Studies, 47*(3), 537–550.

Weick, K. E. (2015). Ambiguity as grasp: The reworking of sense. *Journal of Contingencies and Crisis Management, 23*(2), 117–123.

Weick, K. E., & Ashford, S. J. (2001). Learning in organizations. In F. M. Jablin & L. L. Putnam (Eds.), *The new handbook of organizational communication: Advances in theory, research, and methods* (pp. 704–731). Thousand Oaks, CA: Sage.

Weick, K. E., & Sutcliffe, K. M. (2001). *Managing the unexpected: Assuring high performance in an age of complexity.* San Francisco, CA: Jossey-Bass Publishers.

Weick, K. E., & Sutcliffe, K. M. (2003). Hospitals as cultures of entrapment: A re-analysis of the Bristol Royal Informary. *California Management Review, 45*(2), 73–84.

Weick, K. E., & Sutcliffe, K. M. (2006). Mindfulness and the quality of organizational attention. *Organization Science, 17*(4), 514–524, 526.

Weick, K. E., & Sutcliffe, K. M. (2007). *Managing the unexpected: Resilient performance in an age of uncertainty* (2nd ed.). San Francisco, CA: Wiley-Blackwell.

Weick, K. E., Sutcliffe, K. M., & Obstfeld, D. (1999). Organizing for high reliability: Process of collective mindfulness. In R. I. Sutton & B. M. Staw (Eds.), *Research in organizational behavior* (Vol. 21, pp. 81–123). Stamford, CT: JAI.

Weick, K. E., Sutcliffe, K. M., & Obstfeld, D. (2005). Organizing and the process of sensemaking. *Organization Science, 16*(4), 409–422.

Weick, K. E., & Westley, F. (1996). Organizational learning: Affirming an oxymoron. In S. R. Clegg, C. Hardy, & W. R. Nord (Eds.), *Handbook of organization studies* (pp. 440–458). London: Sage.

Wildavsky, A. B. (1988). *Searching for safety.* New Brunswick, NJ: Transaction Books.

Young, K. (2016). *Exploring organizational resilience asset and its antecedents for effective internal crisis communication.* Baton Rouge, LA: Louisiana State University.

Zaumane, I. (2016). The internal communication crisis and its impact of an organization's performance. *Journal of Business Management, 12*, 24–33.

Zerfass, A., & Franke, N. (2013). Enabling, advising, supporting, executing: A theoretical framework for internal communication consulting within organizations. *International Journal of Strategic Communication, 7*(1), 118–135.

Zimmerman, R. (2013). Crisis communications. In B. K. Penuel, M. Statler, & R. Hagen (Eds.), *Encyoclopedia of crisis management* (Vol. 1, pp. 188–193). Los Angeles, CA: Sage.

Index

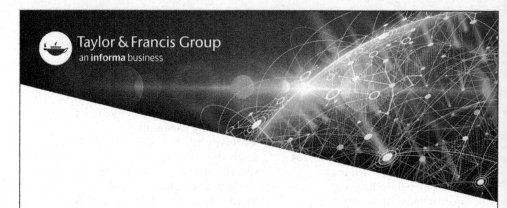